# A GUIDE TO

# Poems of Sylvia Plath

## PAT LEVY

*WITH TONY BUZAN*

Hodder & Stoughton

Cover photograph ©: Corbis UK Ltd
Mind Maps: Ann Jones
Illustrations: Karen Donnelly

ISBN 0 340 75321 8

First published 1999
Impression number    10 9 8  7 6  5 4  3  2  1
Year                 2002  2001 2000 1999

The 'Teach Yourself' name and logo are registered trade marks of
Hodder & Stoughton Ltd.

Typeset by Transet Limited, Coventry, England.
Printed in Great Britain for Hodder & Stoughton Educational, a division of
Hodder Headline Plc, 338 Euston Road, London NW1 3BH by Cox and Wyman Ltd,
Reading, Berks.

# CONTENTS

There are five important things you must know about your brain and memory to revolutionize the way you study:

♦ how your memory
('recall') works *while* you are learning
♦ how your memory works *after* you have finished learning
♦ how to use Mind Maps – a special technique for helping you with all aspects of your studies
♦ how to increase your reading speed
♦ how to prepare for tests and exams.

## Recall during learning
### – THE NEED FOR BREAKS

When you are studying, your memory can concentrate, understand and remember well for between 20 and 45 minutes at a time. Then it needs a break. If you carry on for longer than this without a break your memory starts to break down. If you study for hours non-stop, you will remember only a small fraction of what you have been trying to learn, and you will have wasted hours of valuable time.

So, ideally, *study for less than an hour*, then take a five to ten minute break. During the break listen to music, go for a walk, do some exercise, or just daydream. (Daydreaming is a necessary brain-power booster – geniuses do it regularly.) During the break your brain will be sorting out what it has been learning, and you will go back to your books with the new information safely stored and organized in your memory banks. We recommend breaks at regular intervals as you work through the Literature Guides. Make sure you take them!

# Recall after learning
## – THE WAVES OF YOUR MEMORY

What do you think begins to happen to your
memory straight after you have finished learning something?
Does it immediately start forgetting? No! Your brain actually
*increases* its power and carries on remembering. For a short
time after your study session, your brain integrates the
information, making a more complete picture of everything it
has just learnt. Only then does the rapid decline in memory
begin, and as much as 80 per cent of what you have learnt can
be forgotten in a day.

However, if you catch the top of the wave of your memory,
and briefly review (look back over) what you have been
studying at the correct time, the memory is stamped in far more
strongly, and stays at the crest of the wave for a much longer
time. To maximize your brain's power to remember, take a few
minutes and use a Mind Map to review what you have learnt
at the end of a day. Then review it at the end of a week, again
at the end of a month, and finally a week before your test or
exam. That way you'll ride your memory
wave all the way there – and beyond!

# The Mind Map ®
## – A PICTURE OF THE WAY YOU THINK

Do you like taking notes? More important, do you like having to
go back over and learn them before tests or exams? Most
students I know certainly do not! And how do you take your
notes? Most people take notes on lined paper, using blue or
black ink. The result, visually, is boring! And what does *your*
brain do when it is bored? It turns off, tunes out, and goes to
sleep! Add a dash of colour, rhythm, imagination, and the whole
note-taking process becomes much more fun, uses more of your
brain's abilities, and improves your recall and understanding.

A Mind Map mirrors the way your brain works. It can be used
for note-taking from books or in class, for reviewing what you
have just studied, and for essay planning for coursework and
in tests or exams. It uses all your memory's natural techniques
to build up your rapidly growing 'memory muscle'.

You will find Mind Maps throughout this book. Study them, add some colour, personalize them, and then have a go at drawing your own – you'll remember them far better! Stick them in your files and on your walls for a quick-and-easy review of the topic.

### HOW TO DRAW A MIND MAP

1 Start in the middle of the page. This gives your brain the maximum room for its thoughts.
2 Always start by drawing a small picture or symbol. Why? Because a picture is worth a thousand words to your brain. And try to use at least three colours, as colour helps your memory even more.
3 Let your thoughts flow, and write or draw your ideas on coloured branching lines connected to your central image. These key symbols and words are the headings for your topic. Start like the Mind Map on page 3.
4 Then add facts and ideas by drawing more, smaller, branches on to the appropriate main branches, just like a tree.
5 Always print your word clearly on its line. Use only one word per line.
6 To link ideas and thoughts on different branches, use arrows, colours, underlining, and boxes (see page 7).

### HOW TO READ A MIND MAP

1 Begin in the centre, the focus of your topic.
2 The words/images attached to the centre are like chapter headings; read them next.
3 Always read out from the centre, in every direction (even on the left-hand side, where you will have to read from right to left, instead of the usual left to right).

### USING MIND MAPS

Mind Maps are a versatile tool – use them for taking notes in class or from books, for solving problems, for brainstorming with friends, and for reviewing and working for tests or exams – their uses are endless! You will find them invaluable for planning essays for coursework and exams. Number your main branches in the order in which you want to use them and off you go – the main headings for your essay are done and all your ideas are logically organized!

# *S*uper speed reading

It seems incredible, but it's been proved – the faster you read, the more you understand and remember! So here are some tips to help you to practise reading faster – you'll cover the ground more quickly, remember more, and have more time left for both work and play.

♦ First read the whole text (whether it's a lengthy book or an exam or test paper) very quickly, to give your brain an overall idea of what's ahead and get it working. (It's like sending out a scout to look at the territory you have to cover – it's much easier when you know what to expect!) Then read the text again for more detailed information.
♦ Have the text a reasonable distance away from your eyes. In this way your eye/brain system will be able to see more at a glance, and will naturally begin to read faster.
♦ Take in groups of words at a time. Rather than reading 'slowly and carefully' read faster, more enthusiastically.
♦ Take in phrases rather than single words while you read.
♦ Use a guide. Your eyes are designed to follow movement, so a thin pencil underneath the lines you are reading, moved smoothly along, will 'pull' your eyes to faster speeds.

# *P*reparing for tests and exams

♦ Review your work systematically. Cram at the start of your course, not the end, and avoid 'exam panic'!
♦ Use Mind Maps throughout your course, and build a Master Mind Map for each subject – a giant Mind Map that summarizes everything you know about the subject.
♦ Use memory techniques such as mnemonics (verses or systems for remembering things like dates and events).
♦ Get together with one or two friends to study, compare Mind Maps, and discuss topics.

### AND FINALLY...

Have *fun* while you learn – it has been shown that students who make their studies enjoyable understand and remember everything better and get the highest grades. I wish you and your brain every success! –(Tony Buzan)

# HOW TO USE THIS GUIDE

This guide assumes that you have already read at least a few poems by Sylvia Plath, although you could read 'Background' before that. It is best to use the guide alongside the poems. You could read 'Themes' without referring to the poems, but you will get more out of it if you do refer to them to check the points made, especially when considering the questions designed to test your recall and help you think about the poems.

The 'Commentaries' section can be used in a number of ways. One way is to read a poem and then read the commentary on it, referring to the poem. Then read the poem again to see how it has changed for you, and how well you now understand it. When you come to a test section, test yourself – then have a break!

'Topics for discussion and brainstorming' gives topics that could well feature in exams or provide the basis for coursework. It would be particularly useful for you to discuss them with friends, or brainstorm them using Mind Map techniques (see p. vi).

'How to get an "A" in English Literature' gives valuable advice on what to look for in a text, and what skills you need to develop in order to achieve your personal best.

'The exam essay' is a useful 'night before' reminder of how to tackle exam questions. 'Model answer' gives an example of an A-grade essay and the Mind Map and plan used to write it.

## The questions

Whenever you come across a question in the guide with a star ❷ in front of it, think about it for a moment. You could even jot down a few words in rough to focus your mind. There is not usually a 'right' answer to these questions: it is important for you to develop your own opinions if you want to get an 'A'. The 'Test yourself' sections are designed to take you about 10–20 minutes each – which will be time well spent. Take a short break after each one.

# KEY TO ICONS

## *Themes*

A **theme** is an idea explored by an author. Whenever a theme is dealt with in the guide, the appropriate icon is used. This means you can find where a theme is mentioned just by flicking through the book. Go on – try it now!

The threatening nature of everyday life

Death

Motherhood

Bees

Woman and artist

Anger and bitterness

## STYLE AND LANGUAGE

This heading and icon are used in the Commentaries for special sections on how the author's poetic style and choice of words achieve an effect. Of course, when writing about poetry, you will need to comment on this.

Many people know more about Sylvia Plath's tragic life than about her poetry, but in order to understand her poetry it is necessary to know a little about her life. She has been called a 'confessional poet' – because her poems are inspired by her personal life. Her novel, *The Bell Jar*, is an account of her early life, her nervous breakdown and her suicide attempt, and many people who knew her well can identify people closely linked with her in its characters. In her poems she uses personal symbols, significant events and places, but her poetry is more than just a collection of personal events with which we are invited to sympathize.

Sylvia Plath was born in Massachusetts in 1932, the daughter of a university lecturer whose special subject was bees. She and her family lived near the sea and by all accounts led a very happy life. Her mother dedicated herself to looking after Plath's father, who was very strong-willed and refused to see a doctor, even though he was ill with diabetes. Her father died suddenly when she was 8 years old and her life changed. Her family had to deal with his loss and with financial hardship. They moved away from the seaside and afterwards Plath described this part of her life as if it were a ship in a bottle which she could see but could not reach. Two years later she nearly drowned in an accident.

She studied hard and won scholarships to good schools, where she received lots of prizes and was very happy. When she was 21 she got a job as a guest editor on a New York magazine, but then returned home exhausted. After failing to get a place on a writing course, she became depressed and attempted suicide, hiding beneath the house to give the sleeping pills time to work. Fortunately her brother found her in time and she slowly recovered from her depression in hospital, where she received electroconvulsive therapy.

She went back to college and gained a two-year scholarship to study at Cambridge in England. There she met, fell in love with and quickly married Ted Hughes. They were both poets and read each other's work and encouraged each other. After some years of travelling they settled in Devon. Sylvia had a little girl and then a miscarriage, quickly followed by appendicitis. After a year or so the couple had a son.

Her marriage got into difficulties, ending when she discovered that Hughes was seeing another woman. During this time she deliberately drove her car off the road – but was not badly hurt. Plath stayed in the cottage in Devon for a time and wrote her best poetry, all within the space of a few months, getting up each morning before the children woke and writing sometimes several poems a day. Her unhappiness seemed to free her poetic genius.

When the spell of inspiration ended she went to live in London with the children. She found a flat and moved in during one of the coldest winters on record. She lived there for only a few months, becoming more and more unsettled before making a third suicide attempt. This one was successful. People who knew her have said that they didn't think it was a genuine attempt – that she must have wanted to be found.

After her death, and partly because of it, her fame as a poet grew and lots of people became interested in her life story. Because many of her poems chart the complexities of her life and question what it means to be a woman, she became a symbol to women who were also questioning their role in society and the limits which society put on their lives.

If you are interested in Sylvia Plath's life story you might like to read *Birthday Letters*, a collection of poems written by her husband Ted Hughes, about their marriage.

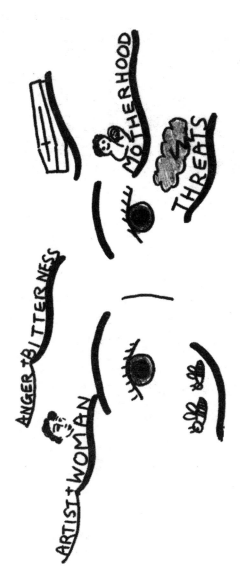

A theme is an idea developed or explored throughout a work. The main themes of Sylvia Plath's poems are shown in the Mind Map on page 3. Test yourself by copying the Mind Map, adding to it, and then comparing your results with the version on p. 7.

The major details of Plath's life described under 'Background' have all contributed to the themes which we can pick out in this selection of her poetry.

## Death

As we have seen, her father's death and her own suicidal feelings played a large part in her life. This emerges in many of her poems and can be seen even in this tiny selection, in 'The Arrival of the Bee Box', 'Wintering' and 'Stings'. In some of her poetry such as 'Stings' and 'Lady Lazarus' she extends the idea of death to one of rebirth where the poet is able to recreate herself through some deathlike experience. This links up with the theme of herself as a woman and a creative artist.

## Bees

We know that Plath's much-loved father was an expert on bees and it is no coincidence that she should have written a whole series of poems about bee-keeping. Bees became for Plath a very personal symbol of her life. We will look at this symbol more closely later on. The queen bee in particular became a symbol of her own empowerment and her genius as a poet. In some of her poems, the swarm represents anger.

## Birth and motherhood

For Sylvia Plath nothing was simple. In many of her poems she looks at the contradictions in her life between her role as a dutiful daughter, a mother and wife and her duty and rights as a creative artist. In the poems in this selection which deal with child-bearing, 'Metaphors', 'You're', and 'Morning Song', she is quite at home with her motherhood, yet there are still some sombre elements in these poems where doubts about her role appear.

## Bitterness and anger

Sylvia Plath went through periods of great bitterness and anger
in her life, particularly at the break-up of her marriage. We can
see this, for example, in the poem 'Sting', where the strange
figure of the man appears and where she talks of the years of
her life which she feels she wasted. In poems such as 'Lady
Lazarus' and 'Cut' the mood of the poem is bitter and angry
but the poetry is not about that anger. In 'Cut' she sees men as
a series of agents or victims of violence.

## Woman and artist

Sylvia Plath grew up at a time and in a community in which
most women saw their role in life as that of wife and mother. If
you had lived then you might have used expressions like 'lady
doctor', 'woman lecturer', 'poetess' to describe women who
did jobs other than traditional women's ones. In a letter Plath
recalls how her husband says she is a fine 'woman poet' as if
women who wrote poetry were a different kind of poet to
men, rather inferior but making a good stab at it. Many of her
poems look at her role as a poet and, in some, her poems
become her children and the tortured process of writing them
becomes a kind of birth. In 'Lady Lazarus' she examines her
role as a woman, comparing herself to a side-show exhibit,
one who can die and be reborn as a new and more powerful
woman while in the poem 'The Applicant' she looks very
cynically at the role of a woman as a wife and declares that
she is no more than a series of functions – carer, sex object,
protector.

## The threatening nature of everyday life

What part of her life led to this aspect of her writing is less
clear but there are many examples of this theme – in
'Mushrooms', 'Mirror' and in the bee poems and
'Blackberrying'. Normal everyday things take on a strange and
vaguely disturbing aspect. In two of the poems here Plath

achieves this effect by giving a voice to the inanimate objects about which she is writing. In 'Mushrooms' the vegetables are part of some conspiracy, while in 'Mirror' the poem's subject takes on a cool, seemingly objective voice, judging the emotional woman from a distance and making her seem more pathetic and fragile as a result.

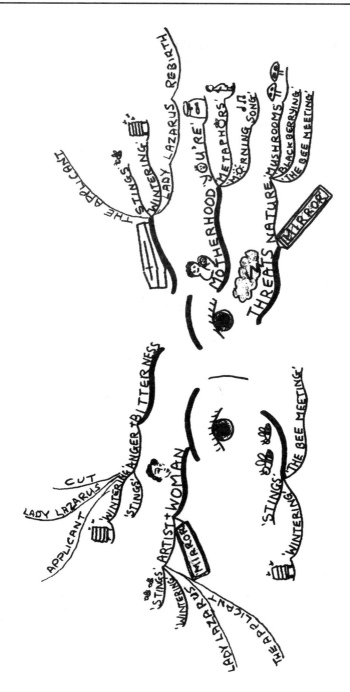

# STYLE AND IMAGERY

As a young woman Sylvia Plath was very ambitious to be a writer and often tailored the style of her writing to suit the publisher to whom she was sending it. She thought of herself primarily as a novelist, and who knows what direction her writing might have taken once she had the passionate poems of her last book of poetry, *Ariel*, off her chest. This fluctuating style of writing emerges in her poetry. It is as if she is playing with poetic styles to see which one suits her best. It is worth noting the different styles she adopts in this selection.

## Metre

Traditional English poetry since the time of Chaucer is written in a fairly regular rhythm which closely mimics the pattern of our heartbeat – five beats to every breath we take. This is called **iambic pentameter**. A line of it looks like this (the dashes mark the stresses):

/   /     /       /       /
*To last it out and not come back at all*

This is a line from the poem 'Lady Lazarus'. It is perfect iambic pentameter and if you read it aloud you will hear that every other syllable is a stressed one. This is the metre which Shakespeare chose for his sonnets and which many more poets have adopted. There are five stressed syllables to a line. But a poem which has a rhythm as regular as this in every line tends to sound rather like a nursery rhyme, and while that jingly rhythm suits nursery rhymes it can sound odd and even insincere in a love poem or a poem describing some beautiful countryside. What distinguishes good poetry (among other things) is the poet's ability to adapt the metre to her needs. In the later poems in this selection Sylvia Plath is using this traditional form of metre. It is a little chopped about and not always in lines of five stressed syllables, but it is easy to hear it if you concentrate.

In her early poetry Sylvia Plath experiments with other metrical systems. Poetry before Chaucer tended to count syllables whether they were stressed or unstressed so a line of poetry had to have an exact number of syllables, usually with four stressed syllables, two in each half of the line. A good example of this kind of metre is in 'You're':

/      /       /  /
*Feet to the stars, and moon-skulled,*

/       /    /      /
*Gilled like a fish. A common sense*

/     /       /  /
*Thumbs down on the dodo's mode*

Most of the lines in this poem have eight syllables with two pairs of stressed syllables in each half of the line. 'Mushrooms', 'Metaphors' and 'You're' all use this syllable counting and replace a regular rhythm with lots of **internal rhymes** (rhymes within lines rather than at the ends of lines) and **alliteration** (where a consonant sound is repeated, especially at the start of words).

There are often times in these three poems when we can hear the natural rhythms emerging through the syllable counting of the lines. It is usually when the poet expresses something passionate or energetic. So, in 'Mushrooms', in stanza 10 when the mushrooms are telling us how they have this power to take over the world we hear:

/  _  _  /  _
*Nudgers and shovers*

_  /    _  _  /
*In spite of ourselves*

Here the rhythm is very regular, this time in a slightly different, faster rhythm called **trochaics** where there is a pattern of one stressed and two unstressed syllables. When you write about Plath's poetry in an exam you should be able to talk about how she uses rhythm to create the style that she wants but just saying what the rhythm is won't get you any marks. You will get marks if you can show how the rhythm is part of what Plath wants to say. As we look at each poem we will try to focus on this aspect of each one and say how you can use it effectively in an exam.

# Rhyme

Another aspect of Plath's style is the use of rhyme. In traditional iambic pentameter or some other rhythmic pattern, rhyme often comes at the ends of the lines in various patterns. The effect of this can occasionally be to add to the nursery rhyme quality. Shakespeare sometimes used rhyming couplets when he wanted to make the speaker sound insincere or stupid. Plath never really used end-rhymes, but especially in her early poetry she put half-rhymes or full rhymes within the lines of the poem. But by the late poetry this rather contrived use of internal rhymes is less prominent as she turns away from syllable counting and internal rhyme to what must have felt more natural to her, loose rhythmical lines and occasional rhymes. We will look at her use of rhyme more closely in the commentaries.

# Choosing the right word

Sylvia Plath spent hours looking through a thesaurus when she first began to write poetry. In a thesaurus you can look up the word you are thinking of and find words which have roughly the same meaning. What she was doing was looking for a word which carried her meaning and sounded right too. So in 'Mushrooms' we get *Soft fists insist on / Heaving the needles*. If you think of the sound or movement of mushrooms pushing up through the soil, the sounds that these words make seem to echo it. They are all soft, pushy noises. There are no hard syllables here which might be more like a sudden striking movement. The word 'heaving', with the 'h' like an expelled breath and the long 'e' noise, mimics the movement of heaving, and could therefore be called **onomatopoeic**. It is echoed in the same 'ee' noise in needles. In the same poem *nudgers and shovers* is a different sound. If we could translate sound into movement it would be a quick furtive movement.

Having said this, please be very careful what you put in an exam answer about the sounds of words. 'Heave' might sound like heaving but, 'weave' or 'leave', both almost the same sound, don't sound like the actions they represent! Notice, by the way, that Plath could have written 'heave the leaves' but doesn't. ✪ Why do you think that is?

These commentaries look at each poem in turn, focusing on its meaning and underlying themes, and on its style and language. You will get more from the commentaries if you refer to the poems as you read them.

## Icons

Wherever there is a focus on a particular theme, the icon for that theme appears in the margin (see p. ix for key).

You will learn more from the commentaries if you read each poem before reading its commentary, and if you refer to the poems as you read the commentaries. In addition, do not simply regard the poems as 'translation exercises'; no study guide can give you a precise meaning for a poem. Remember, too, that you will get marks in the exam for your own thoughts and feelings about a poem, providing you back them up with evidence.

## Questions

Remember that when a question appears in the Commentary with a star ✪ in front of it, you should stop and think about it for a moment. And remember to take a break after completing each exercise!

# Mushrooms

In this poem some mushrooms talk about themselves and their place on earth. Look in your fridge and see if there are any mushrooms in it. Better still, go to the supermarket and look at and touch the white field mushrooms on sale there. ❂ What do they look like to you? What do they feel like? Do they seem alien or frightening?

In this poem Plath is taking a fairly ordinary everyday item, the mushroom, and giving it a vaguely threatening quality. It sounds silly to suggest that mushrooms are frightening, but by giving the mushrooms a voice and human qualities such as intentions she gives us a completely different perspective on them. Read the poem through once. ❂ What do you notice about the shape of each stanza and the line length?

### *STANZAS 1 AND 2*

These two stanzas, each consisting of three lines of five syllables each make up the first statement of the mushrooms. These are strange creatures which have toes and noses and go about their business of pushing up into the air very quietly.

❂ Since we know that mushrooms don't have toes or noses, what do you think Sylvia Plath means by this? What are the similarities between a small mushroom and a toe or a nose? Listen to the sounds of the first two stanzas. Do you notice any pattern of sounds?

### *STANZA 3*

The mushrooms tell us that no one sees them grow or stops them from growing. They insinuate that their growth is secret by saying *Nobody … betrays us*, as if they might be caught out and stopped if anyone did notice them. The mushrooms are part of a conspiracy; they are growing secretly with some insidious motive that no one knows about. In stanza 1 there were repeated 't' sounds', and in stanza 2, 'o' sounds; here the sound pattern includes the repeated 'us' and lots of 's' sounds. This gives their speech a sneaky, whispering sound.

### STANZAS *4, 5, 6*

The mushrooms talk to us quietly and smoothly, not pausing to stop, as if their message has to be passed on quickly before anyone notices. Now they have fists, but not hard masculine fists. Theirs are soft like a baby's and can move the pine needles and leaf litter of the forest as well as finding a way through cracks in the paving. This is a well-observed point about mushrooms – they are soft to the touch and yet are able to find their way through to paved suburban streets. Perhaps it is this quality that made Plath think of the theme for her poem.

In stanza 5 the mushrooms have tools – hammers and rams, and whereas before they had human qualities, now they seem to be deformed, without eyes, ears or voices. They have none of the higher intellectual capacities of humans, and they are becoming grotesque as well as sneaky. ✪ What do you think their secret plan is?

### STANZAS *7, 8, 9*

Now we learn about a new aspect of these insidious creatures. We have learned about their silent, night-time creeping amongst us; the way they insinuate themselves into places, and their great force despite their softness. Now they have made themselves useful to us so as to disguise their threat. They are tables or shelves, they can be eaten and don't need to be fed. But by their force of numbers, strength and secrecy they are unstoppable.

### STANZAS *10, 11*

In stanza 10 we learn that their nature is almost against their own will. They grow and multiply in spite of themselves. By morning they will have succeeded and will survive and multiply after humankind has gone. Their secrecy is stronger than our ability to survive and there is no stopping them since now they have a foothold. Notice the biblical echo in the second line: 'Blessed are the meek. For they shall inherit the earth' (Matthew 5:3) ✪ Why do you think Plath uses this quotation?

In a way these mushrooms seem to symbolize something very unpleasant that Plath feels about the world in which she lives;

that sneakiness and subversion are stronger than boldness and forthrightness. ❷ If these mushrooms were people what kind of people do you think they might be?

Part of her horror of the mushrooms stems from their simplicity. They are a lower form of life but they will dominate the world. Intelligence and a superior mind are no guarantee of survival. In a way this poem isn't about mushrooms at all, but about Plath's feelings towards the world.

It may also be relevant that in the late 1950s and early 1960s Plath attended the mass rallies of the Campaign for Nuclear Disarmament. Like many intellectuals of her generation and those after, she had a pessimistic outlook on the future of the human race. For many people the mushroom cloud generated by nuclear explosions came to represent the future.

### Over to you

?     On page 16 is a Mind Map of the poem. Compare it
      with the poem and see if you would want to change it
      to suit the way you see the poem. Or perhaps you
      think some things need to be added. Using it, see if
      you can retell the words of the mushrooms.
?     Which of the following words do you think we can
      apply to the mushrooms?
      sneaky, forthright, troubled, ruthless, sad, attractive,
      resourceful, useful, wicked, surprised

### STYLE AND LANGUAGE

This poem uses lots of internal rhymes to achieve its effect. There are several different types. When two words rhyme completely such as 'overnight' and 'white' it is called 'full rhyme'. Find all the examples of this in the poem and write them down.

Another form of internal rhyme is **assonance**. This is when the vowel sounds of words rhyme but the consonants around them do not as in *hold* and *loam* in stanza 2. Find other examples of this in the poem now.

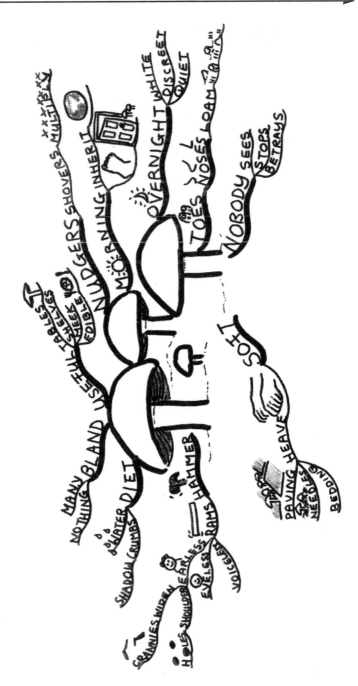

Other types of rhyme are also used in this poem. Some words almost rhyme such as *Whitely* and *quietly* or *Acquire the air*, while in others only the unstressed syllables rhyme such as *Whitely, discreetly*. In some places the rhymes or assonance come at the end of the lines:

*Our toes, our noses*
*Take hold of the loam*

In others places an end word of one stanza rhymes or almost rhymes with an end word of the next:

*Earless and eyeless*

*Perfectly voiceless,*
*Widen the ...*

In the exam you will get no credit for merely pointing out the forms of rhyme the poet uses – only for showing how she uses it to get her effect. We have already mentioned the sibilant, hissing, whispering sounds of the mushrooms. On other occasions the internal rhymes or near-rhymes help to package the poem more tightly together. They also work with another stylistic device that Plath uses – making one stanza run on to another, which technically minded people call **enjambment**. Similarly you will get no credit just for pointing out enjambment – you must show how and why it is used.

Here the overall effect of the rhymes and the pace of the poem is to package the poem together, to make the mushrooms seem more conspiratorial, as if they are deliberately choosing their words. Unlike more traditional poems which have a regular rhythm and end-rhymes to hold the poem together, this one uses internal rhymes and half-rhymes.

Sometimes Plath is just playing with the sounds of the words!

One more literary term before we leave 'Mushrooms' and go on. When a poet takes an inanimate object and gives it a voice or makes it seem alive it is called **personification**. We do this in everyday speech when we say 'the wind howled' or 'the bus lumbered along the road'. We give animate, often human qualities to inanimate objects. In this poem Sylvia Plath achieves her effect by personifying the mushrooms – giving them human qualities. Or more truthfully she is telling us about some human qualities she despises and fears by imposing them on these mushrooms. Again you get no credit for the jargon but rather for showing why she adopts this stylistic feature.

*take a break before moving on to the next poem*

## Metaphors

This poem is written like a riddle – a very old form of guessing game. One ancient riddle, the riddle of the Sphinx, is: 'What has one voice, and walks on four legs in the morning, two at noon and three in the evening?' The answer is – man! He walks (crawls) on four legs as a baby, in the morning of life, on two legs as an adult in the noon of life and uses a stick in old age – the evening of his life. Morning, noon and evening are used as metaphors for life's stages. ✪ Think of other riddles you have heard

Before we begin to look at this poem, read it through. There are nine lines and each of them is a metaphor or a group of metaphors representing the same thing. ✪ Can you guess what it is? Another thing to notice before we begin to look more closely is the number nine. The poem has nine lines and each line has nine syllables. A clue is in the number if you haven't yet guessed the answer to the riddle.

The riddle is, of course, a pregnant woman. No marks for guessing that one! What is more interesting is to look at the narrator's metaphors for her condition so that we learn just how she feels about it.

### LINE 2

First she is an elephant, then a ponderous house. An elephant is huge and very strong and its movements are usually very slow while a house is a place of safety. This house is a ponderous one – it moves slowly and thoughtfully. She is imposing her own ponderous feelings and slow movement on the house. ✪ Do you think she is enjoying being pregnant?

## LINE 3

Her next riddle deals with another aspect of her physical state – she feels like a melon balanced on two tendrils. Tendrils are fine, fragile plant stems which easily snap. A melon has a thick, fairly hard rind, but inside it is red and soft and watery. If a melon falls it smashes open on the ground. ✪ What does this tell us about how she feels?

## LINE 4

The next line is *Oh red fruit, ivory, fine timbers!* ✪ Is this a new riddle? In fact it is an exclamation of joy using the three metaphors that have gone before. It is a shout of appreciation at the fine timbered house, and the contrast of the red, sweet fruit and the white of the ivory. These are of course also the colours of blood and bone, the building materials of the narrator herself and the child growing inside her.

## LINE 5

Next she is a loaf of bread which rises as it bakes. Here the metaphor calls up the smell and taste of bread as well as its physical similarity to her swelling body. It conjures up images of warm, welcoming kitchens and a wholesome life.

## LINE 6

In the next line the narrator is a purse full of newly minted coins. We get the sense of the satisfaction and comfort of holding a purse full of money. The baby growing inside her is like new money. It isn't yet worn and handled like ordinary money or people who have lived part of their lives. Here the baby is like wealth stored away for the future. These last two lines are clearly very positive about her pregnancy.

## LINE 7

The next line is a quick string of related ideas; the narrator is a means (and here we finish the idea for her of 'a means to an end'), a stage in the baby's development and then a pregnant cow. These are slightly less positive metaphors for her condition. Her importance in the world right now is only as a stage in someone else's life story. The narrator feels like an unintelligent and ungainly creature, just a piece of livestock.

### LINE *8*

These rather difficult ideas lead to the idea of having eaten a bag of green apples – she has stomach pains – a metaphor for the pains of childbirth perhaps or the feeling that she has been a bit greedy and is now going to suffer for it. We could even stretch the idea of the apples to the Eden story where Adam and Eve ate the fruit of the Tree of Life and were thrown out of the earthly paradise. The baby represents a loss of innocence and paradise for her. Her life will no longer be simple and easy – it will be full of responsibility.

### LINE *9*

The last metaphor, of someone getting on a train that she must remain on to the end of the line, conveys her feelings of not being in control of what is happening to her. She chose to have the baby of her own free will, just as the passenger got on the train, but now she can't change her mind. She just has to sit and passively wait for whatever might happen while she is pregnant and for the rest of her child's life.

So, while this poem is mostly quite positive about this period of expectant motherhood there are some ambiguous thoughts towards the end of the poem. There is both hope and apprehension in her string of metaphors.

Notice that there is very little playing with rhyme or the sounds of words as there was in 'Mushrooms'. ✪ Do you think that this makes this a better or worse poem?

### Task time

?     Re-read the poem and draw your own Mind Map. See if it agrees with the one on page 21. Perhaps yours is a better version!

?     If you happen to know a woman expecting her first baby, read this poem to her and ask if she agrees with it.

?     How can you tell from this poem that this is the poet's first baby?

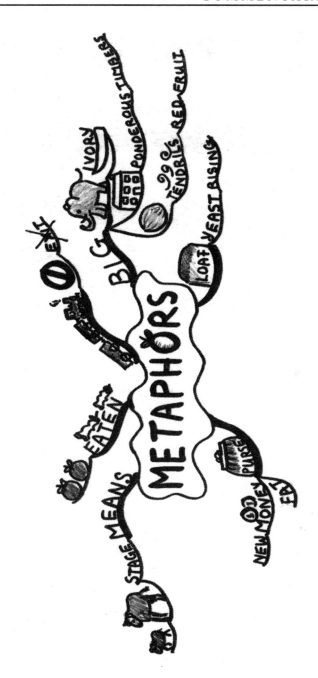

**?** Which of the following statements about the poem do you agree or disagree with, and why?

In this poem a woman expresses her hopes and fears about her future.

In line 3 she expresses her sense of physical fragility.

Her pregnancy makes her feel big and ungainly.

She wishes she wasn't pregnant.

There is a sense of loss as well as happiness.

She feels that events are taking over and she is no longer in control of what is happening.

**?** This poem uses a metrical pattern of syllable counting rather than the traditional English poetic use of regular rhythms. Read the poem aloud. Can you hear any recognizable patterns of rhythm? If you can, what do you think the rhythm is adding to the poem? Look particularly at the last line.

*take a break to think of a riddle*

## You're

This poem belongs to the period of Plath's first pregnancy and uses a similar metrical style to the first two poems we have looked at: it counts syllables rather than having a regular rhythmical pattern.

Like 'Metaphors' it lists a set of images, in this case to describe the unborn baby. However, here the images are more sophisticated. The things to which the baby is compared are down-to-earth everyday items not usually associated with poetry – such as the turnip in stanza 1. Yet these images are elusive; it is hard to say exactly what they mean. They hint at much more complicated ideas than those found in 'Metaphors'.

The poem is more complex in other ways too. It uses lots of rhymes and half-rhymes and often breaks into discernible rhythms as well as the syllable counting. ✪ Read the poem through once and write down all the things you understand about how Plath feels about this baby. Note all the bits you're not clear about.

## STANZA 1

Look at the first sentence of the poem. It lasts through two and a half lines. ❍ If you didn't know that this was an unborn child she was talking to, what would give you a clue? The child is clownlike. Perhaps she is thinking of circus clowns walking upside down as comfortably as upright. The child inside her is in this position – head down, with its feet to the stars. *Gilled like a fish* reminds us that the child is floating in amniotic fluid, its lungs full of liquid yet breathing in its own way. ❍ Why do you think she chooses the moon to describe its head? Why choose the word *skull* rather than 'head'?

The metaphors she is choosing are very light-hearted; her developing baby is a happy creature, at home in its environment. The stars and the moon here seem hopeful things which suggest a happy future for the child. The moon parallels the shape of the child's hairless, developing head. In some of her more morbid poetry the moon represents something worrying and dangerous, and a skull is a universal image of death, but here there is no suggestion of that.

The next metaphor runs across one and a half lines of the stanza. It is less clear than the those of 'Metaphors'. The thumbs down is a very down-to-earth way of saying no to something and it also copies the shape of the developing foetus, upside down with its limbs tightly held against its body. What the *dodo's mode* means to the poet is less clear. Perhaps she is thinking of the flightless bird which wasn't able to survive or adapt or perhaps it is the simile 'dead as a dodo' which she is recalling. It stresses that the baby is happily alive and surviving and will be able to adapt to its new life. Again the metaphor is tightly packed with lots of suggestions, and is very positive.

The idea of the upside down fist leads to the next figure of speech. This time Plath chooses a simile, which is often a much simpler way of expressing an idea than a metaphor. A metaphor is like a double exposure on film. Two things are compressed together and it takes a certain amount of effort on the reader's part to unpackage them and see what the two things are. In a simile the two objects are held up for us so we can look at each of them and see the similarities. Most of the remaining images are also similes. This one compares the baby to a spool, a roll – of film or cloth. The baby is wrapped up in itself – preoccupied with itself, but also literally wrapped up, in its own arms.

Still part of the same sentence (although again there is no main verb) is the simile of the foetus as an owl. The word *trawling* (fishing with a drag-net) again recalls the idea of the child floating in fluid. This time, however, the foetus is like an owl which can fly (unlike the dodo) and has sharp eyes, flying along looking for prey, perfectly adapted to its environment. The owl reminds us again of the stars and moon, and the darkness in which the foetus lives.

The next three lines focus on the growth of the baby inside her. It is silent *as a turnip*. Perhaps it is the shape of the vegetable which suggests itself, or the idea of it sitting in the soil over the winter slowly growing. The child is quiet, perhaps just waiting its time to reveal itself. If you count out the months from July to April it comes to nine. ❂ Why do you think the poet chooses these two festivals as the period of the child's gestation?

In fact Frieda was born on 1 April but the two dates are very happy ones in the calendar. The Fourth of July is America's Independence Day when there are parties and firework displays, and 1 April is a time for playing tricks and enjoying life. This links up with the idea of the baby as a circus clown playing tricks. The baby is keeping silent till All Fool's Day when it will emerge into the world, already full of tricks to play on its parents. It is also spring, when the countryside is beginning to revive.

The last line is part of the same chain of ideas, all connected with the growth of the foetus. It has exactly the same tone and pattern as line 4 in 'Metaphors' – a great exclamation of joy. It mirrors 'Metaphors', too, by using the image of the loaf rising, but this time the metaphor applies to the child not to the pregnant woman. She seems particularly proud of her child, which is rising high, perhaps suggesting a successful future for the child.

## STANZA 2

The next stanza changes direction a little to introduce the woman's feelings of expectation. Two similes come first, again packed tightly together. The child is *vague as fog*. ❷ What do you think are the similarities between an unborn child and fog? Plath helps us out a little by telling us that it is the vagueness of the child that reminds her of fog.

What this simile conjures up are her feelings of expectation. Wondering what her child will be is like looking for something in thick fog. You can just make out the outlines of it but you can't quite see it properly. As the object approaches through the fog it gets clearer until when you are right beside it you can see it. The second half of the line is also about her sense of expectation. It is like waiting for the postman to bring a hoped-for letter

The next two lines extend this idea of the child being so near her and yet so inaccessible. Now it is *farther off than Australia*, the farthest place on earth from where Plath was when she wrote this. Australia suggests the idea of Atlas, the mythological figure who carried the burden of the world on his shoulders. This returns to the shape of the foetus inside her, curled up but as strong as Atlas. The *travelled prawn* again recalls the idea of an incompletely formed foetus as well as the image of distance that the baby must travel before it will be with them. The word *our* in this line suggests the idea of the expectant parents waiting together for the arrival of the baby.

The next group of similes all pour out mixed up together and go back to the idea of the baby tucked up comfortably in the womb. *Snug as a bud* makes us start a little because we read the first three words and want to finish it with 'bug in a rug' but the word used is bud. This suggests the traditional simile but adds to it with the idea of the child all folded up and waiting to bloom. Again she stresses the child's ease and well-being but with a very peculiar image of a *sprat in a pickle jug*. In Plath's poetry things inside jars are usually a bad sign, like dead specimens in a laboratory, but this time the fish is happy inside the jar. A *creel* is a fishing basket or trap made from cane, and so the similarity to the *creel of eels* is a new idea of the child wriggling about like eels in a basket. This idea of movement leads her to the idea of a Mexican jumping bean and her own experience as the child moves inside her.

The last two lines sum up her expectations for the baby. It is right, as when your maths teacher ticks a sum done correctly. The child is complete, with no errors or complications. The idea of the schoolroom puts her in mind of a blackboard or the old-fashioned slates on which children used to write. The expression 'a clean slate' means that the past has been put aside and things can start anew. When this child is born it will be a completely new start.

This is a happy, positive poem about Plath's future child. There is no sense of being out of control as there was in 'Metaphors'. It is light-hearted and humorous, and the similes and metaphors tumble over one another as they pour out, leaving no time or room for verbs, except for the one in the title. It is strange that two very potent images from other parts of her work, the moon and things in jars, both often used as symbols of death and inability to change, are used here with no associations of unhappiness.

### Over to you

?     What can you say about how Plath uses rhyme and metre in this poem? Can you see a reason for having two stanzas rather than one long poem?

?     Make a Mind Map of this poem.

?     Finish and explain each of the following similes:

Gilled like a ...
Mute as a ...
Vague as ...
Snug as a ...
Jumpy as a ...
Right, like a ...

Do these similes have anything in common?

*now take a break before we look at the last of the poems in this selection about motherhood*

# Morning Song

This poem was written about a year after the birth of Frieda and after the miscarriage of her second pregnancy and it marks a change in tone between the optimism and fun of the previous poem and the more serious nature of this one. It was the poem Plath chose to begin the collection of her poetry called *Ariel* and it begins on an upbeat note with the word 'love'.

Read the poem and write your own version of what she says to the child that she has now known for about ten months.
❂ How has the tone changed from the last poem to this one?

### STANZA *1*

This stanza describes the arrival of the child into the world. The child is compared to a gold watch, which is set ticking by an act of love. Fat gold watches conjure up ideas of comfort and wealth so the first image is a very comforting one of love and wealth. Strangely though, the narrator doesn't bring herself into these first moments of the child's life. The mother had nothing to do with the child's beginnings – it was *Love*. At the birth the midwife is there with the child but the mother doesn't seem to feature in the event.

### STANZA *2*

In this verse the parents of the child are mentioned. She pictures the child as a new exhibit in a museum, a statue which the parents just observe. The parents have become *blank as walls*. The child represents a kind of threat to the parents – *your nakedness/ Shadows our safety*. Somehow the presence and vulnerability (*your nakedness*) of the child throws a shadow over the safety of the parents. ❂ Can you explain why this would be the case?

### STANZA *3*

The narrator explains the way in which she has portrayed the new child so far in the poem. First of all the woman who stood in wonder in the museum in stanza 2 denies that she is the child's mother. It is as if she is saying that this creature is so complex and amazing that she couldn't be its mother, or at least she doesn't feel as if she is. Then she explains why she feels so distanced from the child – using a long, complex image to do it.

In this image the poet sees herself as a cloud which rains and makes a pool of water. In producing the pool the cloud destroys itself (since it was a collection of water vapour), and the mirror made by the pool reflects the gradual dissolution (*slow effacement*) of the cloud. It is a kind of **allegory**, in which elements of a story represent other things. If the narrator is the cloud then producing the child (the pool) has become her own destruction since all her creative energies must go into the child and she will wither away as a person.

The feelings of the parents and the threat posed by the baby become clearer with this image. When parents look at their children they see future generations, but they also see for the first time their own death and their own vulnerability.

## STANZA 4

But then halfway through this poem the tone changes completely and Plath's humour and feelings of maternal love for the baby reassert themselves. She moves from these strange dream landscapes – the draughty museum and the pool of water – to a very real, warm situation. It is night, and the narrator lies awake listening to her child's faint breaths. It is a very domestic scene with a pattern of pink roses on the walls. The woman listens to the sounds of her child sleeping, hearing the noise of the sea in her ear. Perhaps here for a few minutes she is remembering her happy seaside childhood. It is a pleasant, calm scene. Notice how the phrase *moth-breath* mimics the tiny breathing noises of the child.

## STANZA 5

The child suddenly wakes and cries and the narrator automatically moves to comfort it. Here she is *cow-heavy and floral*. With this description of herself, which we have met before in 'Metaphors', she is able to laugh at herself and her ungainliness in her voluminous flowery nightie. There is no romantic Madonna-and-child imagery here, no beautiful glowing mother caressing a perfect child. The child's mouth is open and it seems as clean as a cat's – again another quite startling and unusual simile to describe the open mouth of the child. The stanza flows on to the next one, where we see the mother looking out of the window as dawn comes, the stars gradually disappearing. The child's cry becomes a series of balloons rising up into the sky.

 In this poem the writer's experiences of ten months of the reality of child-rearing, plus the sadness of losing a baby, have altered the glee and humour of the earlier poem. She sees now that the child means she is losing part of herself. There is a balance between the sense of parental responsibility and the love she feels for the child.

There is also a balance between the closeness of the mother and child, with the mother moving automatically to meet the child's needs, and the sense of distance from which she hardly feels any connection with it at all, as if she were a bystander in a museum looking at a new exhibit.

## STYLE AND LANGUAGE

This poem actually looks different compared to the three others. Its stanzas each consist of three lines, just like 'Mushrooms', but here the lines are of uneven lengths. There is no syllable counting, although there does seem to be a rough pattern of long and short lines interspersed. But if the poem isn't syllable counting, it isn't exactly iambic pentameter either. If you mark the stressed syllables over the first couple of stanzas you will notice that while there is no fixed pattern or line length there are little runs of rhythm, so that the first line is:

/    _  _ / _   _  _ / /   /
*Love set you going like a fat, gold watch*

This is a very rhythmic line and echoes the ticking of the clock or the pace of the child's heartbeat.

In the next stanza, where the poet is expressing her sense of distance from the child, the rhythms decline, and commas and full-stops break up the natural pace of the lines. If you look at lines 1–2 there is a full-stop after *New statue* where no stop is necessary, grammatically speaking.

The next stanza returns to a rhythm of a kind but this time it is slower and balanced to match the sentiments. Read the lines aloud to listen to the rhythm of the verse:

> /            /
> I'm no more your mother
>
>        /        /  /        /        /
> Than the cloud that distils a mirror to reflect its own slow
>
>   /            /  /
> Effacement at the wind's hand.

The punctuation and pace of the rhythm allow the image to flow in a single movement. Look at the pace and rhythm of the rest of the poem and try to say how they add to the meaning of what the poet has to say.

One more point to note is the use of verbs. We saw in 'You're' how Plath dispenses with them in the quick playful stream of images describing her child. In this poem we have verbs and it is interesting to notice that the tense changes. In stanza 1 she is looking back at an event – the child's birth – and the verbs are in the past tense. When she goes on in the next stanza to picture how she and her husband felt about the child, the tense alters to the present. This helps to place the scene in an imaginary figurative world. The rest of the poem continues in the present tense but now the use of it makes the scene more immediate as if the events are happening as she speaks rather than being a moment that she is remembering.

### Your turn

?   Look at the Mind Map of the poem on page 32 and decide if you agree with it. Can you add to it?

?   Make a copy of the branches of the Mind Map, leaving out the words. Then cover this one and see how much of it you can remember.

?   Complete the figures of speech and try to explain what you think Plath was thinking of.

1 ............................................. Like a fat gold watch
2 ............................................. as walls

**31**

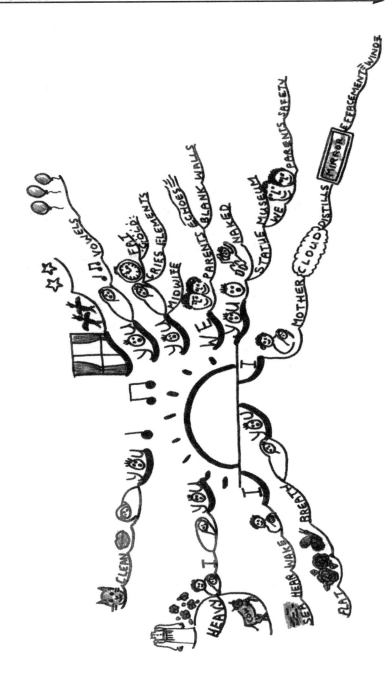

3 Clean as a ......
4 ........................................................ like balloons

These are all examples of what kind of figure of speech?

**?** A metaphor takes two things, such as the fluttering of a moth's wings and the sound of a baby's breath, and fits them together so that the one idea explains or gives a new viewpoint on the other. What things are paired in each of the metaphors below, and how do they enhance one another. The first one has been done for you.

**1** *All night your moth breath / Flickers among the flat pink roses*

Here the two objects mixed together are the sound and movement of air caused by the baby's breathing and the sounds and movements of a moth's wings. It increases the feeling of the delicacy and vulnerability of the child.

**2** *... The window square / Whitens and swallows its dull stars*
**3** *... New Statue. / In a draughty museum ...*
**4** *... A far sea moves in my ear.*

**?** Re-read stanza 3 and explain the allegory in it without looking back at the explanation.

*take a break before picking your way through 'Blackberrying'*

# Blackberrying

It is an old tradition among country families to go blackberrying. But in this poem the blackberrying becomes a solitary and unnerving event. First read the poem and write a brief summary of its events.

## STANZA 1

A woman enters a country lane and sees bushes laden with blackberries leading down towards the sea, although she cannot yet see the sea. She starts to pick the blackberries and puts them into a milkbottle. Simple enough! But just as in the other poetry it is the way in which Plath describes this event that we need to look at, in order to understand what the moment signified for her.

The poem starts off in a very negative way – *nobody ... nothing, nothing ...* But there is something: the blackberries. These get mentioned three times in three lines of poetry. It is as if they dominate everything in the lane. The second line is rather odd for a poem:

*Blackberries on either side, though on the right mainly,*

This seems very ordinary, prosaic language for a poem and the fact that the blackberries are growing more densely on the right side doesn't seem to add much to our picture or understanding. Perhaps she is simply reporting events as they actually happened or she wants to give the poem that sense of a real place rather than a landscape of the imagination. The sentence continues into the next line, giving a clearer picture of the lane. It is like an alley descending down to the sea, and the brambles on which the blackberries grow are like hooks. Hooks are found on the end of fishing lines; they cut into the skin and pull the prey along against its will. An alley is a narrow walled lane with no exits except at either end. So already we have the impression that she is being drawn painfully along this lane rather than going willingly. The sea at the end doesn't seem too promising either: it is heaving.

So in reality we have a simple country lane with blackberries growing on either side and the sound of the sea in the distance but in the poet's imagination it is an enclosed, entrapping place drawing her downwards to a disturbed, as yet unseen, sea.

Then the poet turns her attention to the blackberries again, placing the word at the end of a line so that the automatic pause you make as you read the lines highlights the word. They are huge – as big as the ball of her thumb. This is a very everyday kind of simile but then it is followed by a more distinctive image. The blackberries are dumb as ebony-coloured eyes in the bushes. She pictures them as the eyes of some silent (and stupid?) animal lurking in the hedge, looking at her.

As she picks the blackberries the fruit breaks and the juice stains her hands. She pictures it as blood and the fruit becomes animate, personified as she describes the spilt juice as being squandered. The fruit becomes female as she imagines a blood sisterhood – just as in stories of native American tribes when two men become blood brothers by pricking their hands and mingling their flowing blood.

The blackberries have become rather unsettling and unwelcome friends – people that want her to be a part of them. As she puts them into the milkbottle she says they help her, accommodating themselves to the shape of the bottle. In Plath's imagery things inside bottles often represent death – like specimens in a laboratory in formaldehyde. These berries gladly become like this, which disturbs her.

### STANZA 2

This pleasant, quiet country lane seems to have taken on a strange, unsettling quality for Plath. Here she is talking about her feelings rather than the lane itself. She moves in this stanza from the berries to the surrounding countryside. Above her, choughs – big black birds, are *cacophonous* – making ugly grating noises. Notice the onomatopoeia of *black, cacophonous*. Then she says they are like bits of burnt paper. If you have ever had a bonfire in the garden and burned old paper or cardboard you will recognize the way that still-burning bits of paper float up into the sky and are carried about by the wind.

The cacophonous noise becomes a protest and the repetition of the word echoes the sound. It reminds her of the sea and she fears that she will never see it. The sea has become a threatening object in this strange walk, but yet she has to find it. The fields beyond the lane seem to glow.

Now the berries have become decaying objects, covered in bluebottles and forming a Chinese screen as the iridescent wings of the insects catch the light. The flies have been stunned by the sweetness of the berries. ✪ Does she think that this is what the berries want to do to her? The stanza ends with another hook, reminding us that she is being drawn along this lane rather than choosing to walk down it.

### STANZA 3

Finally we come to the sea, through two hills which seem too green to be near the sea. The sea in this poem is a wild, disturbing thing and yet the fields close to it are lush and fertile. One more hook and she sees the sea, with orange rock cliffs. The sea is nothing, an absence of anything rather than the purpose of her journey. It is just a great space and a noise like silversmiths beating at a metal that they cannot change.

A strange poem. She seems trapped and horrified by the lane with its almost nauseating berries, and yet when she comes to the release of the open air and the sea, it is nothing, colourless and noisy. The hope of a sense of release from the stultifying nature of the berries that want to be her friend, which drug the bluebottles, and which draw her along the lane with their hooks, is unfulfilled. Instead there is something empty and intractable.

# Themes

This poem has a similar theme to 'Mushrooms': in both poems there is an implied threat in the nature of the objects she is writing about. Here Plath takes a perfectly innocent country lane and imbues it with a malice which is aimed at her. Images that she uses in other places crop up here too. In an earlier poem the idea of washing flapping in her face is quite welcoming and domestic, but here it is another threat. The idea of blood recurs in lots of her poetry and is another threatening image. Here the blood sisterhood disgusts her. In her novel *The Bell Jar*, the heroine feels she is trapped inside a glass jar in a laboratory and cannot connect with reality and this idea of dead things in jars is repeated here with the berries going gladly into the jar. And the poem ends with the sea, not the pleasant seaside of her childhood but a vast, shapeless thing.

 ## STYLE AND LANGUAGE

Plath has left behind the syllable counting of her earlier poetry. If you mark the stressed syllables of your copy of the poem you will find that there are lines of fairly even length with four or five stressed syllables on each line with an uneven number of unstressed syllables. Often her poetry becomes quite rhythmical, as in

/        /        /        /      /
*Big as the ball of my thumb and dumb as eyes*

or

/      /        /        /      /
*I do not think the sea will appear at all*

Similarly, while there is no obvious rhyming scheme, she uses internal assonance, alliteration or half-rhymes. We already have *thumb* and *dumb* above and there are lots of other examples.
❂ List as many internal rhymes as you can from the poem.

Another stylistic device she uses in this poem is the repetition of words. English is full of synonyms and when a clever wordsmith like Plath repeatedly uses the same words there must be a reason! The poem begins with a repeated *nothing* and ends with it too, and there are lots of repetitions of the word *blackberries*. ❂ What other words are repeated? Why do you think she might have done this?

### Boost your learning

? Copy the Mind Map of the poem's images on page 38. Each main branch represents something used figuratively. Add a second level of branches for the second item in the image, and a third for the effect it has. One branch has been done for you.

**?** Score each of the following statements about the poem 0–5 according to how far you agree (5 = total agreement). Think about the reasons for your scoring.

1 The narrator goes blackberrying in a lane leading down to the sea.
2 There is no one else in the lane and she feels scared.
3 There seem to be black-eyed creatures lurking in the bushes.
4 She cuts her finger on one of the brambles.
5 The lane seems confining and dark.
6 From the start there is the hope of the sea as a kind of promise.
7 She has a sense of disbelief at how green the fields are.
8 When she sees the sea the sense of space and freedom turns out to be a threat.
9 Blackberry juice looks exactly like blood.
10 There are no happy moments in this poem.

*take a break and look for some sickly blackberries, or anything else in your garden which disturbs you*

## Mirror

This poem resembles the earlier poems in that it takes on the persona, or character, of an object without actually naming it. Notice that in 'Mushrooms', 'Metaphors', 'You're' and 'Morning Song' the subject of the poem is never named in the body of the poem, and only in 'Mushrooms' does the title give it away. This is like 'Mushrooms' in that the title names the object. ✪ If you took the title away, could you guess the subject?

Read the poem through and note what you think is happening here. In the poems we have looked at so far Plath has given us a startling new angle on an everyday object. ✪ How far do you think she is doing the same thing here?

### STANZA 1

It is important to decide in the first few lines if the mirror is telling us the truth. The mirror says that it is *Exact*, that it reports exactly what is there without any alteration. But this is a Plath mirror and we need to be aware of that as we read on.

*I have no preconceptions* – the mirror doesn't judge, it just records. It goes on to tell us, rather smugly, that it reflects everything without judging it or allowing its own emotions to affect what it reflects. It says it isn't cruel, just truthful. ✪ Do you begin to wonder why a mirror would want to tell us these things in the first place, if it is so impartial? Our first real clue that this is a smug, opinionated, self-satisfied mirror is the next description: *The eye of a little god.* The mirror sees itself as a god.

The mirror goes on to record its existence, on a wall in a room. But this mirror has a heart. In the long years that it hangs in the room, day and night and people coming and going seem to be momentary flashes.

### STANZA 2

Now the mirror picks out one particular person. ✪ Is there any physical description of the woman? Is she a happy person? The woman stares into the mirror at her own face, trying to understand what she is. The woman is dissatisfied with what she sees. She turns to *those liars, candles and the moon.* ✪ How are candles and the moon liars? But the mirror keeps on reflecting something the woman doesn't like and she weeps and waves her hands. ✪ Why?

Back to the mirror. It self-importantly tells us that it is important to her. It returns to the passage of time, telling us that the woman changes as the years pass, losing the face of a young girl and gradually seeing the signs of an old woman appearing.

Well, yes, that is what happens – people gradually get older and that is reflected in any mirror they look into. No problem. But – *a terrible fish?* She has *drowned a young girl*?

In many ways this poem might be just a cliché – a woman obsessed by her physical appearance, terrified at her gradual physical degeneration. But in that case, why write the poem in this way? The woman in this poem is hardly there – we have no idea who she is or what her thoughts are. All we know is what a mirror tells us about it. Is this about a vain woman or about a cruel, judgmental thing that sees the perfectly natural course of ageing as something horrific? The mirror claimed at the beginning of this poem to be truthful and objective but when it predicts the future of this woman it calls old age *a terrible fish*. The image recalls the earlier lines depicting a woman kneeling at the lakeside looking for the meaning of her life. Now suddenly this horrific fish surfaces.

It is important to ask yourself who or what is making the terrible fish judgement. Is it the vain woman or is it something else? Sylvia Plath was just 30 when she wrote this. She would have started noticing the occasional laughter line or grey hair. Perhaps she was thinking about what it means to be a woman in a society in which women – far more than men – are judged according to their looks. Plath is saying that the idea of old age as something terrible for a woman comes from society, not from women themselves. So the mirror becomes the voice of society, and women the victims.

## Themes

 This poem takes up one of Plath's constant themes: what is a woman for? Having babies and ironing shirts and looking beautiful? Or does she have an existence beyond that? This seems to be a very negative poem, saying that the woman is a victim whose life is just wasting away as her youth and beauty come to an end. But reading it carefully it is the eye of the little god that is really making the judgements and in her later poems, especially in the *Ariel* collection, the woman figure is positive and in control of her life.

 ### *STYLE AND LANGUAGE*

Plath uses mirrors a lot in her poetry. Often they represent women who are only a reflection of their husbands. At other times she is interested in the fact that they represent the truth. Here she has taken the idea and centred the poem around it. The poem is quite rhythmical with lots of trochaic patterns (two unstressed syllables between each stressed one). This stresses the exact, controlled nature of the mirror's words, spoken very concisely. Her use of rhyme is muted, few of the obvious sound repetitions of 'Mushrooms'. ❂ Make a list of all the internal rhymes in the poem. The language itself is by turns poetic – *and an old woman/ rises towards her day after day –* and very prosaic, ordinary – *it is pink, with speckles.*

### *Boost your learning*

? Complete the Mind Map of the figures of speech in the poem on page 42.

? For each of the lines on page 43 on the left find the corresponding prose version on the right. One of the left-hand list is not a prose version of a line of this poem. On what line, of what poem, do you think it is based?

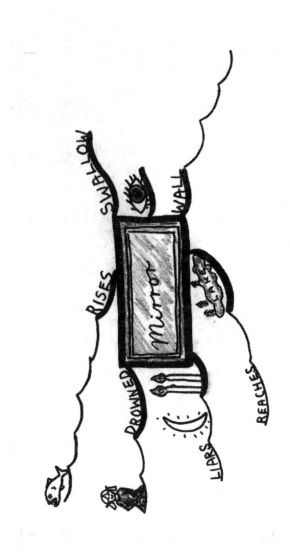

| Quotation | Prose version |
|---|---|
| 1 I have no preconceptions | a Each day as she looks in the mirror the woman sees the signs of old age |
| 2 Whatever I see I swallow immediately | b The woman gets on with her life, occasionally coming into the room to look in the mirror |
| 3 Faces and darkness separate us over and over | |
| | c The mirror is rectangular and thinks it is very powerful |
| 4 Searching my reaches for what she really is | |
| | d The woman prefers to see herself by candlelight or moonlight which is more flattering |
| 5 She rewards me with tears and an agitation of hands | |
| 6 She comes and goes | e The mirror is objective in the way it reflects reality |
| 7 Then she turns to those liars, the candles and the moon | f The woman looks deeply into the mirror at her face |
| 8 The eye of a little god, four cornered | g As soon as someone turns away from the mirror the reflection disappears |
| 9 In me she has drowned a young girl | h What the poet sees is a great space of nothingness |
| 10 in me an old woman/ Rises towards her day after day like a terrible fish | i When she sees signs of ageing the woman gets very upset |
| | j The mirror hangs on the wall for years on end and time is punctuated by the day and night and people's faces |
| | k When she first started to look in the mirror she was a young girl |

*now take a break to check your wrinkles in the mirror!*

# The Bee Poems

In the last months of her life Sylvia Plath was a very angry person, and many critics feel that this released a terrible beauty in her poetry. These four poems come from that period in her life and are very different from the other poems we have looked at. They are all about bees, and we know that her father was a beekeeper and that she herself kept bees in her garden in Devon. The first is set in a weird dream landscape and is an account of an event that really happened, although strangely turned around by Plath's imagination.

# The Bee Meeting

On the most obvious level, this poem is about beekeeping. The villagers are removing the new queen bees before they hatch. If they were allowed to hatch then the old queen would have to leave the hive taking some of the worker bees with her and one of the new queens would kill the others and take over the hive. Plath describes the unhatched new queens as *virgins*, dreaming of killing the others and making this flight. Beekeepers often remove and sell the new queens.

Read the poem through once and note what is happening.

### STANZA 1

The poem starts with a question and then answers it. She is at the bridge in the village and there is a group of people there to meet her, the rector, the midwife, the sexton, and a bee agent. They are typical figures from an English country village. The narrator is wearing a sleeveless summer dress and feels vulnerable in it. All the other people are wearing suitable clothes for beekeeping, hats and scarves with their arms covered against the possibility of bee stings. She asks herself (or us) another question. The event seems a little like one of those dreams where you suddenly find yourself at school or work but in your pyjamas! The people are friendly and smiling and have hats ready to cover their heads. The poem is in the present tense, as if describing things as they are actually happening, giving it an even more dreamlike quality. Plath uses the same technique in 'Morning Song' to describe herself looking at her baby for the first time.

### STANZA 2

Another question follows a very prosaic simile, *nude as a chicken neck*. She feels like a plucked chicken in a butcher's shop with its neck hanging down and pale white plucked skin. The answer to her question is that they do love her. The secretary of bees, perhaps the midwife, finds a shop smock for her to wear. The woman helps her do up the buttons at the cuffs so that the bees cannot get inside and sting her. The smock is white and makes her feel like milkweed-coloured silk. She feels as if she has become invisible to the bees and is now protected. But she is afraid of them and promises herself that they will not smell her fear.

## STANZA 3

Now the other members of the beekeeping society have put on their hats and she cannot tell one from another. Their voices seem to change once they put on their hats. Just as in a dream the woman seems helpless and is led into a field.

## STANZA 4

She describes the beanfield they go into, with strips of tinfoil to keep the birds away, red bean flowers reminding her of blood clots, and heart-shaped leaves. The tendrils of the runner beans seem to be pulling clots of blood up the strings. A sense of threat is emerging here with images of blood, but she tells herself that her imaginings are wrong and that it is just a beanfield.

## STANZA 5

The bee meeting becomes like the initiation ceremony of a mysterious cult. (Remember the horror movies where an innocent young girl is dressed in white and led off to some strange ritual.) They give her a bee hat so she becomes as unknown as they are (or so she won't get stung!) and they lead her into a circle made of bee hives. The hives are kept in a field hedged around with hawthorn, and the perfume from its flowers makes her nauseous.

## STANZA 6

Now her questions are about what will happen. She wonders if they are about to do an operation, and if one of the suited figures is the surgeon. Other village figures may be there now, perhaps the butcher or the grocer or the postman. In their suits they have become mysterious and menacing figures.

## STANZA 7

Now panic takes her over. She is losing her grip on reality and feels unable to move; if she begins to run she will have to run for ever. Finally she focuses on the beehive, which is quietly busy, with the brood cells sealed off and protected. (Brood cells are the part of the hive where the queen bee lays her eggs. Some brood cells produce new queens but others just make regular bees.) The bee society members light a smoker and fill the hive with smoke. (Bees are calmed by smoke and will not sting.) Some bees fly out, ready to fight, and she hopes that if she stands still they will think she is part of the countryside.

## STANZA 8

This carries on with the image of herself as a cow parsley plant, part of the hedgerow, unnoticeable. Meanwhile the others have opened the hive and are searching for the queen. She asks herself more questions about the queen bee and seems to find something in her that she can identify with. The queen bee is old and crafty. She will stay in the hive for another year while the young queen bees are removed by the beekeepers.

## STANZA 9

Plath imagines that the unhatched new queens are dreaming of killing their sisters and making a bride flight. The villagers find the brood cells containing the queen bee larvae and remove them. The narrator wonders if the queen is grateful since she doesn't show herself.

## STANZA 10

The narrator seems to black out for a moment (*pillar of white in a blackout of knives*) She feels like the magician's assistant who has knives thrown at her yet doesn't move. When she comes round, the villagers are removing their beekeeping suits and shaking hands, their work complete. She notices a long white box, presumably for putting the new queens into, and thinks that their operation was conducted on herself, not the bees.

Plath wrote about this event in a journal she kept at the time and the events actually happened but in the poem she translates this simple, fairly everyday country activity into something steeped in symbolism and myth.

Strange hooded figures carry out an initiation ceremony in which the narrator is a victim/unwilling participant. They put a white gown on her. Her passivity and her constant questions make her seem as if she is in a trance and unable to stop them.

In order to sort out the victim/participant problem we need to look at the queen bee in this poem and remind ourselves of the poet's immediate history when she wrote this poem. Her husband had just gone to live with another woman, and Plath felt cheated and betrayed. In this poem the villagers' operation allows the old queen to remain in the hive for another year.
❂ If Plath saw herself as the queen bee, who or what did she equate with the young queen bees? Her description of the old queen bee is interesting: *She is very clever/ She is old, old, she must live another year and she knows it....* and the young queens: *the upflight of a murderess into a heaven that loves her.* The young queen, Plath's rival for her husband's affections, becomes a murderess whom heaven loves.

Sylvia Plath knew that she had to move on as an artist after her marriage ended and this poem isn't a wish that someone would come and sort out her problems but an acceptance that if she is to survive she must become like the queen bee, clever and elusive, and not rely on help (the villagers) which just seems to drug and stifle her.

# Themes

One of the themes of this poem is the poet's survival as an artist. Plath briefly becomes the queen bee in this poem and she knows that her job is to survive and keep her hive. The tone of this poem is quite ambiguous. At the end she doesn't know if she has survived or become a victim of the villagers. The villagers represent something that takes away her vitality and makes her passive, but for a few moments in the poem she empathizes with the queen bee and knows that she must be like her.

In some of her poetry Plath equates babies with poems. Producing a work of art is like giving birth to a child. Here the hive itself becomes Plath's female power and creativity. She tries to fit in with society (the villagers) but realizes that it will drug her and take away her ability to be a creative artist.

This woman feels threatened by the villagers and their intentions. They smile and want to help her but we get the feeling that when she says she is afraid of the bees it is really this foreign society that she is afraid of with their strange rituals and secrets.

Plath was American, a foreigner, an outsider. Here she pictures herself trying to be one of the villagers, dressing like them and letting them initiate her into their society. But her passivity makes her feel vulnerable and drugged and so she fails in her attempt to accept society and its values.

 ## STYLE AND LANGUAGE

We have already looked at some of the imagery used in this poem and noted the constant use of unanswered questions and the present tense to create a sense of passivity and confusion. Stanzas break up the story, although there is one sentence that runs across two stanzas (this is called enjambment, remember). The poem is written in irregular iambics with no obvious end-rhymes but lots of patterns emerging in odd places such as:

> /     /           /      /     /
> *Which is the rector now, is that the man in black?*

> /     /     /     /       /
> *Which is the midwife, is that her blue coat?*

The lines match in metre and pattern of the sentence. Remember we said that too regular a rhythm makes the poem sound bouncy, like a jingle. Here there are little breaks of regular rhythm but not enough to give it that nursery rhyme feel. Similarly the rhymes are subdued, but present if you look for them. We have *milkweed silk, creamy bean, fanning their hands, the mind of the hive,* and a few others, even less obvious. Just as in 'Blackberries' Plath mixes prosaic, everyday images with more traditionally poetic ones so we have the image of herself as a bare chicken neck as well as creamy bean flowers with black eyes and leaves like bored hearts (bored has two meanings – uninterested, and with a large hole drilled through). She also has a mix of similes and metaphors and uses personification for the beans and the bees, giving them human motives. This is a quick list of the poem's stylistic features. Use them to show your understanding of the poem; don't just list them.

**Over to you**

? Complete the Mind Map opposite of the imagery in this poem.

? Fill in the blanks: The narrator is standing by a _____ waiting for _____. She is wearing a sleeveless dress and it makes her feel _____. The people she meets are wearing_____. Her thin, sleeveless dress makes her feel like a _____. But the _____ gives her a _____ to wear. Now she feels like_____. Her overwhelming emotion now is one of _____. All covered in their beekeeping gear the others seem like_____. and their _____ change. They go through a _____ and the flowers remind her of_____. So that she won't get stung they giver her a _____ and a _____. She feels nauseous and blames it on the smell of the _____. The she begins to wonder if an _____ is about to take place. The people open the hive and look for the _____. For a moment the narrator thinks of the queen bee and feels_____. The new queens are dreaming of_____. After the new queens are _____ she blacks out and then notices a_____. She feels _____.

*after that – the most difficult poem so far – you deserve a break!*

## The Arrival of the Bee Box

Read the poem through and note the main events. ✪ Do you get the feeling of an unseen threat from this poem, as in 'Mushrooms', 'Blackberrying' or 'The Bee Meeting'?

### STANZA *1*

The poet describes a clean wooden box, very heavy and square, not coffin-shaped like the box at the end of the previous poem. But it still reminds her of a coffin, perhaps a midget's or square baby's. We are straight into images of death but somehow the square bit adds humour and anyway we are told straight away that it isn't a coffin because of the *din* it is making. This word 'din' suggests badly behaved children rather than threatening monsters. The narrator plays with ideas of death but is detached and curious about the box. Notice also the form of the stanza, short lines, some obvious rhymes, *square ... chair, din ... in.*

### STANZA *2*

She tells us that the box is locked because it is dangerous and she has to spend the night with it in her house. She is drawn to it but can only see in through a little grid in the side. This stanza seems very down-to-earth, almost like prose. ✪ Write it out in a single line and see if it reads like poetry.

### STANZA *3*

She peers in through the grid and sees moving darkness as the bees crawl over one another in an effort to escape. She says it feels like African hands.

### STANZA *4*

In the morning she has to put the hive in its place in the garden and unblock the grid so that the bees can get out to start collecting honey again. She wonders how she will have the courage to let them out. The bees remind her of a mob in ancient Rome, each bee alone presents no threat, just like a Roman citizen, but together they are frightening. Notice the onomatopoeia of *unintelligible syllables,* almost impossible to say but sounding like the angry buzzing of bees.

### STANZA *5*

She puts her ear to the box, and continuing her Roman mob image says she can hear Latin. In ancient Rome Caesar would have come out to the mob and controlled them with promises of bread and circuses but she feels she cannot control these bees in the same way (*I am not a Caesar*). She calls them a *box of maniacs* and sense reasserts itself as she puts aside her fear and tells herself she doesn't have to open the box; she can let them die or send the box back. She makes herself feel as if she does have the power of Caesar and so loses her fear of them.

### STANZA 6

She imagines opening the box the next day and wonders if they will attack her or just ignore her. There are trees in flower and she will be wearing her bee suit so there is no reason to think that they will attack. She feels that tomorrow she will be as powerful as God, with the choice of life or death over the bees.

# Themes

Here again we have the idea of the bee colony as Plath's personal symbol. In this case the colony represents her creative forces and Plath stands outside of it quite cool and confident that she will be able to control it when the time comes. Plath is attracted to the beehive as she is fascinated by her own dark rage.

The bee box is certainly a threatening dark object but there is not the menace here that there is in 'Mushrooms'. These bees are simply angry, not plotting or threatening her personally or the world in general. And Plath is in control of this threat by the end of the poem. In the others the threat is not so controllable. As soon as they are released everything will be normal and they will calm down and go about collecting honey.

 **STYLE AND LANGUAGE**

This is a much shorter poem, more direct with simple imagery which is not as elusive as in the earlier bee poem, It is much simpler in its direct link between the hive and its anger and Plath and her creative energies. There is a sense of humour here in the idea of the square baby and the bees as an angry mob. As in the other poems, rhymes appear at times but they are not the contrived rhymes of the early poems and she does not seem so concerned with form here as with what she wants to say.

Lots of people have seen this poem as a metaphor for the poet's concerns about her creative power. Plath the poet is like the hive of bees, trapped and angry inside the imprisoning role she has played as a wife and mother. In the metaphor, if the hive is opened and the bees (her creative energies and her anger) are let out, she doesn't know if she will have the power to control them. She thinks about her dilemma and decides that she has the power to control whatever will happen when she starts to write down her anger as poetry. She is no longer a passive victim like the helpless narrator of the previous poem.

Often in her poetry black is associated with death but here it is the colour of anger. She uses the image of the bees as African hands shrunk down to a tiny size and climbing all over one another in a swarmy kind of way. She looks into the darkness of the hive and sees all this moving blackness and it frightens her.

**Over to you**

?     Complete and explain the following figures of speech.
square as a.......
It is dark, dark with the........
It is like ..........
I lay my ear to the........
... the petticoats of the ...
Tomorrow I will be ...

?     Why do you think she ends the poem with the single line: *The box is only temporary*.

?     Make a list of all the internal rhymes and try to say what effect they have in the poem.

*brain buzzing? take a break!*

# Stings

Another bee poem, again one that has strange, elusive characters in it, and again one based on a real event. Read it through and write down or Mind Map what is happening here.

### STANZAS *1–3*

The narrator and a man are standing by the hive, bare-headed and with their hands bare too. She and the man are setting up the new hive, shifting the frames of brood cells into her empty hive which she has painted with a pattern of pink flowers. She and the man are described in happy, innocent terms with their wrists like brave lilies and their gloves neat and sweet. They are putting eight frames into the new hive.

The first two stanzas flow as one piece of writing with the *He and I* standing out as a very short line before the second stanza continues the sentence. She is stressing the friendly, companionable relationship between herself and the man who is helping her put the frames into the hive. The same sentence continues into stanza 3 with the word *sweet* echoed in the phrase *'Sweetness, sweetness'*.

The mood changes as she considers the frames of brood cells in her hand. They are grey and look like dead fossils, not live things full of honey and living larvae. She wonders if she is buying worm-ridden mahogany not a honeycomb. And then she wonders where the queen is in these frames.

### STANZAS *4 AND 5*

The queen bee is hidden inside the frames somewhere. The narrator has never seen the queen but she knows it is old, with tattered wings like worn-out shawls and the furry covering on her body worn out like old velvet. A long line describes the queen as poor and bare and unqueenly and shameful and then the next word is *I*. ✪ Is she describing herself or the queen? She then describes herself as one of the worker bees, the sterile females that do all the work in the hive. They have wings but they are *unmiraculous* women, not great poets or painters but creatures who work all their lives to make honey. Then she changes her mind about being a worker bee and tells us she isn't one, although she has been like one for years, carrying out degrading drudgery in the home as wife and mother. She figures her years as housewife as eating dust and drying plates with her hair, the most demeaning and humiliating things she can think of.

### STANZA 6

She continues with a metaphorical account of her history. In all the years of drudgery she watched what was special about her – her creativity – disappear. Then she wonders if these bees, the workers or drudges will hate her. The drudges can only gossip about where good pollen is; they have nothing in common with her.

### STANZAS 7, 8, 9 AND 10

The work she and the bee-seller are doing on the new hive is almost complete. She announces that she is in control and now that she has set up the hive it will work away all summer making honey. But suddenly another figure appears in the story. She tells us that he is an intruder; he has nothing to do with her or the bee-seller. Then he disappears again taking eight great strides like a scapegoat (an innocent person who carries the blame for something bad). The man has left things behind him – a slipper, and a piece of linen. He was *sweet* she tells us, regretting his loss. He tried to help but his efforts were useless and the bees discovered his uselessness and stung him on the lips. This now departed man is considered and then passed by. ❂ Who do you imagine this man might be?

### STANZA 11

When the bees stung the man they died. The poet tells us that the worker bees who attacked the man thought that it was worth dying in order to drive him away, but that she – the poet – has to find herself again. After eight years of marriage she has to become an artist. She wonders where the queen bee is again. She wonders if she is dead or only sleeping and where she has been for all the years that Plath was washing up. This queen bee is no longer a tatty creature but has a lion-red body and wings of glass. She has been reborn.

## STANZA 12

Now the narrator, or queen bee, is flying over the engine (hive/house) that killed her. She is like a comet in the sky, more powerful than ever before. The hive/house is like a mausoleum – a tomb, or wax museum full of dead things – her past.

# Themes

The poem is concerned with the ageing queen bee and her imminent death. Plath has taken up the idea of death and rebirth. In this poem the old queen is reborn as a more vibrant, powerful creature. This comes to symbolize Plath's belief in her ability to be reborn as an artist, so here death becomes a positive thing. Plath rejects the worker bees who give up their lives in a single act of vengeance to protect the hive.

Plath's personal symbol is the queen bee who is rejuvenated or reborn. The hive becomes a symbol of death, first in the grey, wormy looking frames of brood cells, and then in the mausoleum at the end of the poem. The queen bee escapes from the hive and flies about as bright as a comet. This poem is about Sylvia Plath's empowerment as a writer and her rejection of the need for a husband's guidance in her work.

The poem starts pleasantly with the narrator and the bee-seller smiling and innocent. But after she thinks about her wasted years of drudgery the tone changes and she become angrier and angrier until the poem ends with this vital but furious comet streaking across the sky. First drafts of this poem were even angrier and concentrated much more on the scapegoat and his stings.

 **STYLE AND LANGUAGE**

The poem is composed of five-line stanzas. These either stand alone as single ideas, as in the last two stanzas, or flow into one another as the poet's ideas break out of the five-line structure, as in stanzas 1–3. This is the same flowing, loose iambic style which she has used since 'Blackberrying', with occasional internal rhymes loosely holding the poem together but never imposing themselves as the rhymes did in 'Mushrooms'. There are repetitions in this poem too, making it sound like an incantation. Her use of colours is interesting. Most things are colourless, the man's suit, the hive, the brood cells, the creaming crests , the moon, the square of white linen. But the queen bee is red, and the word is repeated – *lion-red … red comet*, contrasting her life and vitality with the deathly white of everything else.

We have seen in this series of poems the change in the narrator/Plath. In the first poem she is helpless, a victim, just momentarily thinking of the queen bee as a figure with which to identify. In the next poem she is in control of the hive, but does not yet make the connection between herself as an artist and the queen bee. Here she makes the connection and in this poem the ageing queen is reborn, more powerful than ever. These poems are about herself and her ability to write poetry, not just about bees.

**Over to you**

? Add to the Mind Map of the poem's imagery, opposite.

? This poem is about the queen bee and her rebirth as a powerful creature. Why, then, do you think it is called 'Stings'?

? Everyone's response to a poem is different. Score each of the following statements about the poem 0–5 according to how far you agree (5 = total agreement). Think about the reasons for your scoring.

The narrator is buying a set of brood cells from another beekeeper.

The tone of the poem is rather unfriendly.

The narrator worries that the brood cells she is buying will not produce a hive.

The queen inside is old and should be replaced with a younger queen.

She resents the years of her life she has wasted on menial work and realizes that it is too late to change.

A scapegoat figure appears and tries to stop the preparation of the hive.

She hates the scapegoat.

The drones killed the scapegoat.

The terrible queen bee represents Sylvia Plath's anger at her failed marriage.

*take a break – how about a honey sandwich?*

# Wintering

Another bee poem, this time a sadder, less positive poem concerning the bees, and Plath in her first winter alone. In her own arrangement of the poems in the volume *Ariel*, Plath put this poem last. Read the poem through and write down what happens in it.

### STANZA 1 AND 2

The poem starts on a positive note. All the work of the hive is over, the narrator has emptied the honey from the hive, spun it in an extractor to separate the honey from the wax honeycomb, and put six jars of honey away in her wine cellar where the amber liquid glows like cat's eyes. The stanza runs on to the next one because the mention of the wine cellar sets her thinking about what it is like. At first her descriptions are fairly neutral. The wine cellar is the heart of the house, has no windows and is full of all the old unwanted things left behind by people who lived there before.

### STANZA 3 TO 6

The heart of the house is a mystery to the poet. She has never been there because when she has tried to go in she couldn't breathe. The blackness in the cellar is *bunched ... like a bat*. The torchlight becomes a faint Chinese yellow and just makes things look worse. There is *Black asininity* in there, a dark stupidity. Notice the single-word sentences. This breaks up the flow of the stanza as well as her thoughts and makes us pause over each word, giving it more emphasis, stressing the unpleasant qualities of the cellar.

Things are decaying in the heart of the house. Already we can see that Plath is talking about much more than a dark cellar. She has named it as the heart of the house and then described it as a rotting, frightening place. Rather than herself owning these unexamined objects in the cellar, they own and control her. She is no longer powerful and vital as she was in the last poem. The things that own her are *not cruel nor indifferent/ Only ignorant*. It is not an evil presence in the cellar, but something stupid and unaware.

This thought leads her on to the bees. Like her, they are hanging on – waiting for winter to end. They fly slowly to the tin of syrup she has left out for them to collect food for the depleted hive.

### STANZAS 7, 8 AND 9

It is deepest winter and snow covers everywhere. The bees are huddled together inside the hive for warmth. She contrasts the black life of the bees with the white smiling snow. Here again we have an ambiguous smile like the smiles in 'The Bee Meeting'. The snow stretches out like a huge piece of Meissen pottery, cold and hard. The bees wait for the warm days to evacuate the bodies of the dead worker bees. Inside the hive there are only women, the queen and her servants. The drones were all driven out of the hive to die when their usefulness was over. ❂ In the line *The blunt, clumsy stumblers, the boors,* is she talking about male bees? Notice the sudden obvious rhymes here. The words seem to sound like heavy-footed men stumbling about. She tells us that men are not necessary in winter; it is a time for women to wait patiently for the spring. The woman, maybe the narrator, sits beside a cradle made of walnut wood, her body drawn into the shape of a bulb. She is unable to think because of the cold. This poem is a long way from the almost joyful triumph of the queen bee's flight in the last poem. The narrator and the bees are just hanging on, waiting for the spring and not sure if they will make it.

### STANZA 10

Her last stanza ends on a series of questions reminding us of the unanswered questions of 'The Bee Meeting'. The narrator really isn't sure about her own chances of survival or those of the bees. But she ends on a positive note, telling us that the bees are flying and they sense that spring is approaching.

# Themes

This is a sadder, more subdued representation of the artist than the previous poem. The glorious comet of the queen bee is now huddled inside the hive and waiting for spring, unsure of her own ability to survive the winter. In Plath's personal symbolism she still identifies with the queen bee but her feelings about her own survival mirror the subdued nature of the bees. Like Plath, the bees now live without males.

 Every day the bees carry their dead out of the hive. Their deaths are mirrored in the decaying things in the cellar and in the natural death of the countryside in winter.

The anger of the previous poem is muted to a sad bitterness in this poem. Men are still rejected utterly, reduced to blunt, clumsy stumblers, but they are gone now and she is reduced to patience and waiting without much hope. It is important though to note that the poem ends on a slightly happier note with the expectation of spring.

### STYLE AND LANGUAGE

In this poem Plath is using the poetic form to express herself, whereas in her earlier poetry she wanted to write poems and thought up subjects for them. Like 'Stings' this poem has a simple form, the stanzas sometimes running on through a sentence as Plath's thoughts extend beyond the five-line form. We have repetitions again with sentence patterns repeated as well as single words.

### Over to you

? Complete the Mind Map opposite for the main threads of thought in this poem. One has been done for you.

? The stanzas concerning the cellar seem a little out of place in this poem about the bees and their survival. Why do you think she included them in this poem?

? Make a list of the internal rhymes in this poem and try to say why they are there.

? Say whether the following are true or false:

The poet is relaxed with no work to do.
She has borrowed a honey extractor from her friend the midwife.
The cellar is full of malevolent creatures and she is afraid to go in there.

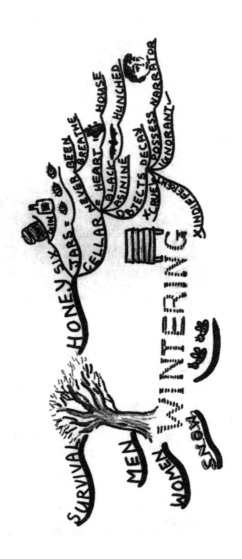

The bees are feeding on syrup from a tin she has put out for them.

There are very few male bees left and a few of them are dying each day.

At the end of the poem the poet believes that spring is approaching and all will be well.

# The Applicant

One of Plath's last poems, written in the bitterness of her anger at the failure of her marriage, this poem is spoken in the tones of a salesperson, selling something to an applicant. Read the poem through and note down what you think the speaker is offering.

### STANZAS 1 AND 2

Before the speaker can get on with business he (❍ or is it she?) must determine if the applicant is suitable, is *our sort of person*. ❍ What exactly determines if the applicant is the right sort? What do the things in the list have in common? What gender do you think the applicant is?

The questioner runs through the list of qualifications and decides that the applicant is not the right sort until he shows his empty hands. Then that makes him acceptable. ❍ Why? ❍ What does the speaker offer him?

### STANZAS 3 AND 4

Running on across the stanza form we learn what is on offer. It is a marriage partner but the woman on offer is less than a woman, just a hand which will perform the functions of a wife. (For collectors of technical terms, this is a **synecdoche** – a figure of speech in which a part of something represents the whole.) Plath shows her disillusion with an ironic black humour which detaches all the complexities of a wife and her feelings from the function that she performs. The woman is nothing but a hand to bring tea, soothe headaches and do what it is told. It will even be there to make the applicant's death tidy – to close his eyes and then dissolve away in tears. The salt from the tears is collected up to manufacture new women.

Next the woman becomes a black suit to protect the man from the many threats which he might meet. The language now is that of a product promotion. We have the repeated *proof … proof … proof* and the glaring end-rhyme of *roof* while the rhythm becomes very regular:

```
_ _  /  _ _      /  _ _      /
It is waterproof, shatterproof, proof
```

```
_   _    /  _  /      _    _  /
Against fire and bombs through the roof
```

The rhythmic quality is suddenly lost in the prosaic *Believe me, they'll bury you in it.* Again, notice the way that Plath comes back to death and burial.

### STANZAS 6 AND 7

Then the woman (*that!*) is brought out of the cupboard and the woman is addressed as *sweetie*. ✪ What effect does this have on us as the readers? ✪ Why choose the simile *naked as paper*? The speaker goes through the investment opportunities offered by this woman. She will grow in value, becoming first silver and then gold. But of course these are just words used to describe wedding anniversaries and really worth nothing. The language of these two stanzas is very up-to-date for the era in which this poem was written, with *ticket*, as in the expression 'just the ticket', *living doll*, and *sweetie*, while the woman has no gender, as if she were a domestic appliance. This is the language of marketing executives.

### STANZA 7

Another list of functions: the woman is a poultice, a sex object, a last resort of the people with the disfigurements listed in stanza 1. The final two verses end in the incantatory repetitions of *talk, talk, talk* and *marry it, marry it, marry it.*

This is a terrible, nihilistic, death-inspired piece of writing but at the same time it has a gallows humour and is a controlled and highly structured work with a clear vision. It reduces human relationships to a series of functions. It suggests that marriage is a last resort of crippled personalities, that women are no more than a set of functions. It illustrates that aspect of

Plath's writing which some critics have called schizoid. Its vision of human relations is at odds with reality (we hope!) like that of schizoid personalities whose view of the world is warped by their emotions. It is the same vision which made Plath write 'Mirror' and describe her married life in 'Stings'.

### STYLE AND LANGUAGE

We see here the deliberate reduction of a woman to a series of functions. Note the use of *it* to name her, and the hand representing the whole body. Note, too, the poet's choice of the language of selling, the repetitions, and the bouncy rhythms like an advertising jingle. All these are part of her central theme – that human relations are a cynical filling of a physical need. The poem is, of course, **ironic**. She does not really see women as merely functional objects. Rather, she grimly ridicules this view of women by pretending to hold it herself.

# Themes

Here she is examining once again woman's role in society. If she feels she is this woman then her strong ideas of herself as the creative writer, symbolized by the queen bee are nowhere in sight or at least they are hidden behind the ironic tone and humour of the poem.

In this interview for a potential marriage partner death is mentioned twice in connection with the woman's uses. It is not so much a main theme of the poem, more an underlying idea, perhaps one that was in the poet's mind at the time.

**Over to you**

? Make a Mind Map of the poem, this time using a separate branch for each stanza. Concentrate on illustrating your Mind Map. What should emerge is a very pictorial diagram. What does this tell you about the poem?

*you deserve a break now – ask your mother to bring you a cup of tea (that's irony!)*

# Lady Lazarus

Lazarus was raised from the dead by Christ four days after he had been laid in his tomb. In 'Stings' the queen bee is reborn as a powerful, young creature and in this poem Plath lays out this idea as the central theme of the poem. Read the poem through and note how she uses this idea of rebirth.

### STANZAS 1–3

We are straight back into the gallows humour of the previous poem here. She tells us that she manages to die and be reborn every ten years. We know from her life story that she almost drowned at 10, and made a suicide attempt at around 20. Here we have her at 30, perhaps contemplating her next approach to death. The tone is wry, upbeat, ironic. She brings in images from Nazi atrocities to describe herself.

### STANZAS 4–5

Carrying on the image of her face as a linen cloth she tells her *enemy* to peel the cloth away and asks if the sight of her decaying face terrifies.

### STANZAS 6–8

She describes the process of the decay of her body and tells that she has to die nine times before it all ends. This she tells us is her third death and resurrection, one for each decade of her life.

### STANZAS 9–12

Here she becomes a sideshow freak with crowds pushing into the sideshow to get a look at her as she is unwrapped like a mummy. We hear the tones of the showman calling the crowds in and describing what they see – hands and knees, just skin and bone but still the same woman as before her death. She relates the various episodes of dying she has encountered, the first an accidental near drowning at age 10.

### STANZAS 13–14

These recall her suicide attempt at age 20 where she tells us she closed in on herself like a closed seashell and people had

**67**

to work hard to call her back to life. She imagines them picking the worms from her corpse in their efforts.

### STANZAS 15–16

The narrator turns to self-mockery, telling us that she is adept at dying. She focuses on what it feels like to die.

### STANZA 17–22

Putting aside the deaths as easy she moves on to the rebirths and says they are the hard part – waking up and finding she is still the same person in the same place with the sideshow crowds standing about and watching the trick. But there is a price to pay for the pleasure of watching her come back to life, listening to her heart beating again, seeing flesh and blood and we know that it is she who pays the price, not the crowds of watchers. Then she addresses the sideshow owner as *Herr Doktor ... Herr Enemy.* The owner who benefits from the sideshow is a man, the concentration camp doctor, a German like her father.

### STANZAS 23–6

She describes herself as a piece of valuable property, just like the disembodied woman in the last poem. Suddenly the sideshow woman begins to burn and is reduced to the parts of her that will not burn – soap like the soap made from the body fat of concentration camp victims, a wedding ring and a gold filling.

### STANZAS 27–8

Now the woman addresses God and Lucifer, addressing them both as Herr, the German name for Mr, so as to establish their gender more intensely and warns them that when she is resurrected she will rise from the ashes and will have red hair (the same colours as the resurrected queen bee in 'Stings'), and will eat men as if they were nothing more than air.

The poem ends on an angry note. The resurrected Lady Lazarus will return to take her revenge on those who have exploited her, and she names them – all male figures. It is important also to note that her wedding ring is one of the three things to survive her consumption by fire. In an interview Sylvia Plath described the woman in the poem as someone '... who has the great and terrible gift of being reborn. ... She is the Phoenix, the libertarian spirit ... she is also just a good, plain resourceful woman.' Having named her enemy as men, this woman can fight back. It is a poem written in that same period of intense anger at men and the society that, as she saw it, condoned their behaviour.

 **STYLE AND LANGUAGE**

The tone of this poem shifts about from sick humour to very modern language (*peanut crunching crowd, What a trash, the big strip tease*) to extreme physical descriptions of rotting flesh, sour breath, worms *like sticky pearls*, to almost triumphant pleasure at her abilities, self-pity and more terrible anger. It is a fast-moving poem, with lots of enjambments, the poet charging on to the climax of her consumption and rebirth.

Imagery is piled up and almost impossible to sort out. First she pictures herself as items of Nazi experiments, then a tablecloth to be peeled away in layers. She becomes the sideshow figure and later, as she describes her earlier death, a seashell covered in worms, then again the concentration camp victim and later a gold baby, a valuable, an opus then a burning corpse and finally the Phoenix being born from the flames.

# Themes

Here she carries on the theme of death into the idea of rebirth, drawing on episodes from her own past and using the violent deaths of the concentration camp victims to express her feelings.

The poem is driven by a fierce humour and anger at the man who has exploited her. Just as in 'Stings' this anger turns into a source of creative energy as the woman imagines her rebirth and revenge.

**Your turn**

**?** How do you think a Mind Map could be used to represent this poem, with its complicated and violent imagery? A branch for each stanza, sentence, image, series of connected ideas, or perhaps for each of the five senses? Draw your own Mind Map of the poem.

**?** The narrator says, *Dying /is an art, like everything else./I do it exceptionally well.* Does this seem to you to be an accurate or valid view of death?

*now do something light-hearted for a while!*

## Cut

Written after the break-up of Plath's marriage this poem, dedicated to a nurse whom she hired to help with the children, retells mockingly the story of a badly cut finger. Read the poem and note all the male figures that appear in it.

### STANZAS 1–2

The protagonist has cut the top off her finger. The tone is lively, inappropriate for the situation and full of everyday speech. As the sense runs over onto the next stanza the language changes to her old playing with sounds, using rhymes and half-rhymes. She observes the cut finger as if it were distanced from her, contrasting the colours of red and white.

### STANZA 3–4

The finger becomes a pilgrim, an early American settler, scalped by Indians. The blood dropping from the cut becomes the red skin of a turkey wattle and it drips straight from the pilgrim's heart. She steps on the blood on the floor.

### STANZAS 5–7

The image of the pilgrim changes to that of a host of red-coated soldiers running into battle as the red drops pour out of her finger. She wonders who the soldiers are fighting for. Her finger becomes a *Homunculus*, a little man. She tells it she is ill – whether from her pain at the cut finger or the pain of her emotions she doesn't say. Next the finger is a saboteur then a kamikaze pilot, both of whom seek to kill or damage.

### STANZAS *8–10*

The images of male war figures grow with the gauze bandage she now has on the thumb being compared to the white hood of a Ku Klux Klan member but she tries to soften that image by making the gauze also a babushka, a head-dress worn by old Russian women. She watches the blood darken on the gauze and mocks the heart's jump at its pained response to the injury. In the final stanza, after all the references to male violence another female image is brought in to the poem with *dirty girl*. The thumb is a war veteran who has had head surgery, then a dirty girl and finally just a thumb stump.

 **STYLE AND LANGUAGE**

Here she adopts a lively style. In some of her other poetry she has seen the flow of blood as the flow of creativity and here she is using this real event where she loses quite a lot of blood to show that it has spurred her ability to write. The poem is constructed around a fast series of images of male violence – a scalped settler, red-coated soldiers, a kamikaze pilot, a racist, an injured war veteran. Her language goes back to her earlier poetry seeking rhymes and half-rhymes as she plays with the sound of words. She uses a four-line stanza form with lines of varying length and no obvious runs of regular rhythm but with a preponderance of two stressed syllables to each line.

# Themes

This lively poem disguises Plath's underlying anger at her life and marriage. All these male figures are violent and she laughs at their antics. In stanzas 6 and 7 when she talks about her feelings they are not caused by the cut thumb but by the terrible thing that has happened to her. Her description *The thin, papery feeling* is followed by the word *Saboteur*. This word describes the man who has, in her opinion, sabotaged her life.

The flow of blood stimulates her creative energies and so she writes this lively, creative piece of poetry. Faced with the betrayal of men and society (as she saw it) she can still create.

Over to you

?  Explain what you think Plath was getting at in the following figures of speech
A flap like a hat
red plush
Little Pilgrim/The Indian's axed your scalp
Out of a gap/A million soldiers run,/Redcoats every one
The stain on your/Gauze Ku Klux Klan/Babushka

?  Make a Mind Map of the poem, showing the use of imagery. Each branch should represent something that she has used figuratively. Make the second level of the branch the thing with which she is comparing it, and perhaps the third level its effect. You should find that a lot of your first stages are the thumb!

# TOPICS FOR DISCUSSION AND BRAINSTORMING

With poetry especially it is very useful to work with a friend or group of friends, either when you read the poem for the first time or when you are revising for an exam. Often one person will understand or notice something that the others haven't and you will get ideas as you talk. Even if your friends don't understand a word of the poem you will find that as you try to explain what you understand things will become clearer to you, you will remember key points in the poem and your thoughts will become clearer.

Try a **brainstorming** approach to the new poem. Having read the poem you should sit down and wait for ideas. Don't think your ideas through before you speak, just let them emerge. Even if you talk nonsense, something good will emerge and your ideas will suggest ideas to other people.

Whether you are working alone or in a group or with a friend, use the **Mind Mapping** techniques described here. It will help you brainstorm ideas and will also help you organize your ideas. Use a big sheet of paper and coloured pens and make each leg of the Mind Map a different colour. You can use Mind Maps to outline the story in the poem (if there is one!) or follow through the themes or the figures of speech. Mind Maps will give you a better overall impression than a list or highlighting the important bits in the poem. Ted Hughes even used them to help him write poems.

Below are some questions which you could consider as you revise and which may come up in the exam itself. Be careful in the exam, though, to answer the specific question given. Don't just assume you can give the same answer that you have worked out here.

### TOPICS

**1** Why do you think Sylvia Plath was so fascinated by bees? What do they represent to her?

**2** Compare two of her bee poems that you have read. Which do you prefer and why?

**3** In her early poetry Sylvia Plath loved to play with the sounds of words. Write about one poem where she does this and say what effect it has.

**4** Which poem of Plath's do you like the most and why?

**5** In the poems about her babies Sylvia Plath has mixed feelings about them. Write about two of her poems about pregnancy or motherhood and show what these mixed feelings are.

**6** In the poem 'Blackberrying' Plath describes an ordinary event in an unusual way. How does she do this?

**7** Give an account of the poem 'Mirror'. Do you think the mirror is telling us the truth about itself?

**8** 'Mushrooms' is about some everyday vegetables but to Plath they become very sinister creatures. Show how and why you think she does this.

**9** In 'Wintering' Sylvia Plath seems both sad and hopeful. Can you explain why?

**10** Sylvia Plath's imagery is often very startling. Pick out two poems where you find the figures of speech interesting and say why.

**11** Compare the poems 'You're' and 'Metaphors' and say how she feels about the future in each of them.

**12** How important do you think it is to know some details of Plath's life before you read the poems? Write about two poems which your knowledge of her life has helped you to understand. Alternatively write about two poems which you think can be fully appreciated without knowing anything about her.

**13** Not long after she had written 'Wintering', Sylvia Plath killed herself. Does this knowledge affect the way you understand the poem?

**14** Write about a poem of Plath's where the dominant tone is one of happiness. What is it that makes her happy? How does she express it?

**15** How does Plath use humour in her poems?

**16** Which do you think is the most difficult of Plath's poems, and why?

**17** Write about a Plath poem that focuses on the countryside or country life. Do you think she likes the countryside?

## In all your study, in coursework, and in exams, be aware of the following:

- **Characterization** – the characters and how we know about them (e.g. what they say and do, how the author describes them), their relationships, and how they develop.
- **Plot and structure** – what happens and how it is organized into parts or episodes.
- **Setting and atmosphere** – the changing scene and how it reflects the story (e.g. a rugged landscape and storm reflecting a character's emotional difficulties).
- **Style and language** – the author's choice of words, and literary devices such as imagery, and how these reflect the **mood**.
- **Viewpoint** – how the story is told (e.g. through an imaginary narrator, or in the third person but through the eyes of one character – 'She was furious – how dare he!').
- **Social and historical context** – influences on the author (see 'Background' in this guide).

## Develop your ability to:

- Relate **detail** to **broader content, meaning and style**.
- Show understanding of the author's **intentions, technique and meaning** (brief and appropriate comparisons with other works by the same author will gain marks).
- Give **personal response and interpretation**, backed up by **examples** and short **quotations**.
- **Evaluate** the author's achievement (how far does the author succeed and why?).

## If studying a poem, look for:

- the **emotional tone** (sad, sombre, lively, confused …);
- the **subject** and underlying **theme or themes**;
- the **structure** and **rhyme scheme** (if any), and the use the poet makes of them – remember you will get credit for saying what they are used for, but not for just identifying them;
- effects made by the **choice of words**, and by **imagery**.

# THE EXAM ESSAY

## Planning

You will probably have about an hour for one essay. It is worth spending about ten minutes planning it. An excellent way to do this is in the three stages below.

1 **Mind Map** your ideas, without worrying about their order yet.
2 **Order** the relevant ideas (the ones that really relate to the question) by numbering them in the order in which you will write the essay.
3 **Gather** your evidence and short quotes.

You could remember this as the **MOG** technique.

Then write the essay, allowing five minutes at the end for checking relevance, and spelling, grammar and punctuation.

**Stick to the question**, and always **back up** your points with evidence in the form of examples and short quotations. Note: you can use '. . .' for unimportant words missed out in a quotation.

## Model answer and plan

The next (and final) chapter consists of a model answer to an exam question on Sylvia Plath together with the Mind Map and essay plan used to write it. Don't be put off if you think you couldn't write an essay as good as this one yet. You'll develop your skills if you work at them. Even if you're reading this the night before the exam, you can easily memorize MOG technique in order to do your personal best.

The model answer and essay plan are good examples for you to follow, but don't try to learn them off by heart. It's better to pay close attention to the wording of the question you choose to answer in the exam, and allow Mind Mapping to help you to think creatively.

Before reading the answer, you might like to do a plan of your own, then compare it with the example. The numbered points, with comments at the end, show why it's a good answer.

# M ODEL ANSWER AND ESSAY PLAN

## QUESTION

**The poems 'Metaphors' and 'You're' are essentially about the same thing. Compare and contrast Sylvia Plath's feelings, style and imagery in the two poems. Do they have the same theme?**

## PLAN

Your Mind Map should include a branch for each aspect of this question – feelings, style, imagery and theme. From these branches, use a separate sub-branch for each poem. From this you should notice the similarities and differences. It might be an idea first of all to do a quick Mind Map for each poem so you don't leave anything out of the overall Mind Map.

From this we can draw up a rough outline of the essay. A useful model for all essays is:

- Tell them what you're going to tell them.
- Tell them.
- Tell them you've told them.

**1** introduction – similar subject but different attitudes, differences in style, differences in imagery, etc. (tell them what you're going to tell them!).

body of essay (tell them!)

**2** Feelings. differences and similarities. Give examples.
**3** Imagery – similarities, differences. Lots of examples.
**4** Other aspects of style – rhymes – similar, syllable counting – similar, verbs – different/same.
**5** The narrator/subject of the poems – different.
**6** Themes. Same but one has sense of ominousness.
**7** Conclusion. They are similar in style and theme but the tone is different (tell them you've told them!).

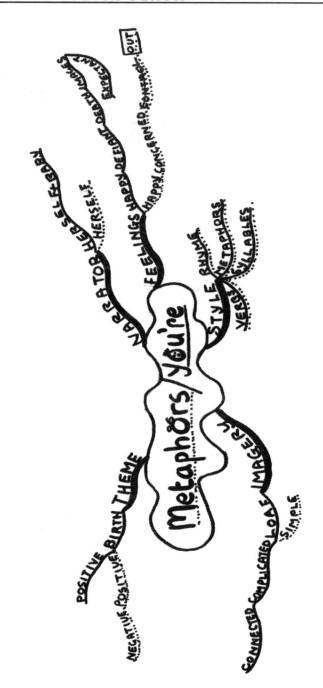

## ESSAY

The two poems, 'Metaphors' and 'You're' are both spoken by a woman who is expecting her first baby. Neither of them actually names the subject of the poem, we just realize as we read who or what she is writing about. Their subject matter is different. One is about how she feels about being pregnant and the other is about her expected baby and how she feels about it. They both share similar feelings and the styles of the two poems are the same but one is a much happier, more carefree poem than the other.[1]

In 'Metaphors' her feelings change as the poem goes on.[2] She begins comically and happily, saying she looks awkward and feels huge

'An elephant, a ponderous house'[3]

But the similes are positive and in line four we hear her almost shout for joy at the thought of her condition:

'O red fruit, ivory, fine timbers!'

But as the poem goes on her mood changes and gradually becomes apprehensive with the image first of all of herself as just a means to an end:

'I'm a means, a stage, a cow in calf'

then the bag of green apples where she thinks of the pain of childbirth and maybe also her own loss of innocence and finally the idea of being on a runaway train that she can't get down from.

In 'You're' her feelings are much more positive all the way[2] through. She focuses on her unborn child rather than herself and every image she uses to describe it is positive and happy. Even images that would normally be associated with harm or death are positive here.

'Like a sprat in a pickle jug'

Normally Sylvia Plath uses the idea of pickled things in jars to show us an image of stagnation and death but here the sprat is happy and there is no sense of harm associated with it. The basket of trapped eels is also a pleasant image rather than giving us the idea of trapped, thrashing animals.

In both poems Plath uses similes as the main form of imagery.[4] Similes are relatively simple forms of image because the writer names both things that she is comparing. She even uses the same image in both poems – the idea of a rising loaf, in one poem to describe herself and in the other to describe her baby. In 'Metaphors' the similes are very simple ones which can be pictured very clearly:

'A melon strolling on two tendrils'

This graphic simile conjures up an amusing picture of the pregnant woman. Similarly the idea of being on a train and wanting to get off, but not being able to, is very simple and graphic.

In 'You're' the images are much more complicated and interlinked than this. One image suggests another similar one and then something reminds her of what she said earlier and the ideas are all packed tightly together and not so easy to unravel for the reader. In this poem we have to work harder to understand what she means. For example in the first stanza the baby is a clown, then moon-skulled, then a fish, then a thumbs-down sign, and then the dodo gets brought into the image. If we unravel all this we can see that she is thinking of the baby's physical position, upside down and not yet completely formed, as well as its condition, which is happy and confident against the threat of death.[5] Even the idea of death – the dodo, an extinct bird which cannot fly, is quite comic. Later in the same stanza she returns to the idea of flying and says her baby is like an owl hunting in the dark. So the idea of flying returns as well as the idea of the night sky which she first mentions in line 2.

In both poems Plath chooses an interesting style of writing. Both are in stanzas of nine lines and 'Metaphors' even counts out nine syllables for each line and uses nine metaphors to describe her condition. Both use a form of syllable-counting as the basic structure of the poem with a repeating pattern of four stressed syllables in each line, although this does vary a little from line to line. Both are written just as a series of similes, although 'You're' uses more complex forms of imagery too. 'Metaphors' is a slower poem usually with complete sentences while 'You're' has no verbs at all except the one in the title.

Both use the poem as a kind of guessing game and do not name what they are writing about. Both use internal rhymes but there is much more of this in 'You're' than in 'Metaphors'. Perhaps playing with the sound of the words is part of her expression of happiness.[6] The most lively, exciting group of metaphors in my opinion is in 'You're' and also includes lots of rhymes:

> 'Bent-backed Atlas.....
> Snug as a bud and at home
> like a sprat in a pickle jug.
> A creel of eels, all ripples.'

The sounds help to pack the metaphors tighter together and add a rhyming dimension to the funny ideas.[7] When we read 'snug as a bud..' we expect it to end 'in a rug' and mentally add it in, complicating the ideas even more.

Another difference between the two poems is in the voice of the narrator. In one she is self-absorbed and thinking only about herself but in the other her feelings are mostly about her child and her feelings of expectation as she waits for it like a Christmas present.

Similarly the themes of the two poems have much in common, but also have subtle differences. The theme of 'You're' is a wonderful, positive expected baby and the happiness that thinking of it brings. The theme of the other poem is more sombre and reflective, aware that there are going to be problems as well as a baby. The baby itself doesn't figure at all in 'Metaphors'.

So, I think these two poems are very interesting viewpoints on an important part of people's life.[8] 'You're' is more fun and livelier but it ignores, probably quite deliberately, any thought that the baby might be less than perfect. I prefer 'Metaphors' because it is more realistic. She is pleased she is expecting a baby but she knows things might get difficult.

## *WHAT'S SO GOOD ABOUT IT?*

1 Focuses on the question and informs us how it is going to be answered.
2 Focuses on the feelings in each poem in turn.
3 Points are backed up by examples from the text and explained.
4 Moves on to second topic, relates it to both poems and illustrates the points.
5 Shows understanding of the poem's imagery.
6 Personal response.
7 Looks at author's technique.
8 Reassesses the topic and provides a conclusion.

# GLOSSARY OF LITERARY TERMS

**allegory**   a story, elements of which represent other things.

**alliteration**   repetition of a sound at the beginnings of words; e.g. *cow in calf.*

**analogy**   an extended simile (see separate entry), explaining one thing in terms of another.

**assonance**   the rhyming of vowel sounds but not the consonants around them; e.g. *hold* and *loam.*

**context**   the social and historical influences on the author.

**enjambment**   making a sentence run on from one stanza to another.

**foreshadowing**   an indirect warning of things to come, often through imagery.

**iambic pentameter**   verse with five pairs of syllables to a line, with the stress always on the second syllable.

**image**   a word picture used to make an idea come alive; e.g. a metaphor, simile, or personification (see separate entries).

**imagery**   the kind of word picture used to make an idea come alive.

**internal rhyme**   rhymes within lines of verse rather than at the end of lines.

**irony**   (1) where the author or a character says the opposite of what he or she really thinks, or pretends ignorance of the true facts, usually for the sake of humour or ridicule; (2) where events turn out in what seems a particularly inappropriate way, as if mocking human effort.

**metaphor**   a description of a thing as if it were something essentially different but also in some way similar; e.g. *Boarded the train there's no getting off.*

**personification**   a description of a thing as if it were a person; e.g *Strip of tinfoil winking.*

**onomatopoeia**   the use of words echoing the sound they describe; e.g. *cacophonous flocks.*

**prose**   language in which, unlike verse, there is no set number of syllables in a line, and no rhyming.

**setting**   the place in which the action occurs, usually affecting the atmosphere; e.g. a lane.

**simile**   a comparison of two things different in most ways but somehow similar; e.g. *Like a sprat in a pickle jug*

**structure**   the overall pattern of a poem or plot.

**synecdoche**   a figure of speech in which part of something represents the whole.

**theme**   an idea explored by an author; e.g. death.

**trochaic**   verse form with a pattern of one stressed and two unstressed syllables.

**viewpoint**   how a story is told; e.g. through action, or in discussion between characters. The viewpoint may include a narrator's bias or feelings about events.

# NDEX

**Page references in bold denote major character or theme sections**

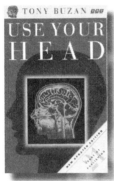